The Job Application
Handbook

8

The Job Application Handbook

Sell yourself to an employer using proven
strategies and effective techniques

JUDITH JOHNSTONE
5th edition

How To Books

Published by How To Books Ltd,
3 Newtec Place, Magdalen Road,
Oxford OX4 1RE, United Kingdom.
Tel: (01865) 793806. Fax: (01865) 248780.
email: info@howtobooks.co.uk
http://www.howtobooks.co.uk

First edition 1993
Second edition 1994
Third edition 1996
Fourth edition 1997
Fifth edition 2000

British Library Cataloguing in Publication Data.
A catalogue record for this book is available from
the British Library.

Cover design by Shireen Nathoo Design
Cover image by PhotoDisc
Cartoons by Mike Flanagan

Produced for How To Books by Deer Park Productions
Typeset by Anneset, Weston-super-Mare, N Somerset.
Printed and bound by Cromwell Press, Trowbridge, Wiltshire.

NOTE: The material contained in this book is set out in good
faith for general guidance and no liability can be accepted
for loss or expense incurred as a result of relying in particular
circumstances on statements made in the book. Laws and
regulations are complex and liable to change, and readers should
check the current position with the relevant authorities before
making personal arrangements.

Contents

List of Illustrations

Preface

to Fifth Edition

When you apply for a job, you are baiting your hook. To get a potential employer to rise to the bait demands proper attention to detail. Only successful applications lead to interviews. Unsuccessful applications are dead ends. So how you approach this crucial first stage is a vitally important part of succeeding in the job-hunting process.

Many job-seekers send out dozens of applications without getting a single interview. They complain bitterly about their lack of success, but the state of the jobs market is not necessarily the reason for their misfortune; the fault often lies in their own hands. Too many job-seekers slam the door in their own faces. Often they do not have the right skills or experience for the jobs they apply for; sometimes they do not bother to research the products or services of the organisations they approach; frequently they tailor their applications to reflect their own needs and not those of the employer, or resort to filling up their applications with irrelevant padding using grand-sounding but meaningless phrases. So what about those dozens of unsuccessful applications? Were they attractive, well thought out, properly constructed products? Or were they nothing more than unfocused, dull or over-blown pieces of prose, lacking anything which might stimulate a recruiter's interest?

Being successful in a fiercely competitive jobs market isn't easy: it takes time and effort. Gone are the days when you could rattle off a brief letter, CV or application form between one cup of coffee and the next: job-hunting has become a skill in itself.

Spurring a recruiter into wanting to know more about you is the secret of success with any application. Each one must be special: it has to be more than just a catalogue of your qualifications or a list of the duties and responsibilities of your previous posts; it has to raise its head above the 50 or more applications lying on the desk of a harassed recruiter; it has to say – 'Here I am. This is what I can offer you.'

This book is designed to help you achieve your goal, whether you are looking for your first opening in the jobs market, returning to work after a career break or redundancy, or simply wanting to move on. It covers essential groundwork; how to organise your job-hunting strategy; in-depth studies of how to tackle letters of application, application forms and curriculum vitae, as well as how to make initial approaches to employers over the phone or by cold-calling.

This updated fifth edition also includes discussions along the way on applications using the Internet. Previously the preserve of engineering, IT and sales job vacancies, this is no longer the case. It is estimated that by 2001 more than half of UK employers will be using the Internet for recruitment advertising. However, Internet recruiting in this country is still in its infancy and there are important factors to be aware of when you use the Net. You should also remember that the Data Protection Act 1998, even when all its provisions are in force in October 2007, will only apply to data within this country, not out there in the global village.

The methods suggested in this book are not meant to be copied slavishly: they are intended to set you thinking about how to present your own skills in an attractive and marketable manner. In the jobs market it isn't the quantity of applications you send out that counts – it's the quality.

Finally, apart from those previously acknowledged for their contribution to earlier editions, I would like to thank the following for providing up-to-date legislation and recruitment information this time around: The City and Guilds of London Institute; the Government Departments DfEE, DTI and especially to Nigel Burke of the Office for the North West; Lakeland Foods Ltd, Kendal; Morecambe Bay Hospitals NHS Trust, Lancaster; HM Prison Service HQ, London; Price Waterhouse Coopers, Belfast; Bay Community NHS Trust, Barrow-in-Furness; Advantage Development Agency, Birmingham; Haswell Consulting Engineers, Birmingham; Briggs Shoes Ltd, Kendal; UK Hydrographic Office, Taunton; NACRO; Apex Trust, as well as staff in the organisations listed under *Useful Addresses* on p.157 and Rob Rod of the 'shadow' Disability Rights Commission who kept me informed of the latest developments.

I would particularly like to thank Tony Taylor of the Chartered Institute of Personnel and Development for taking the time and trouble to explore some Websites with me and for providing background information on the latest recruitment trends using the Net.

Judith Johnstone

1

Preparing the Ground

GETTING YOURSELF ORGANISED

Applying for a job is just the same as starting any other project – it requires good preparation. The success of the project depends on it, whether you are planning a holiday, producing a play or painting the house. The same is true of applying for a job: your chances of success will be greater if you spend time completing the preliminary work properly.

Once you are determined to devote time and energy to the task, making the basic process less tedious should be next on your list of priorities. You must be organised, and to help you achieve this you need two files:

- **a Personal Data file**
- **a Job Record file.**

The aim of this chapter is to help you set up these files so they become valuable working tools in your job search.

There are five good reasons for compiling a Personal Data File. These are:

1. **You have all the facts you need in one place**. This cuts down time-wasting and prevents facts becoming lost between applications.

2. **You have the opportunity to remind yourself of your achievements**. We all have more skills than we give ourselves credit for. Not all will be work-related, but some may be transferable skills, or portable skills to give them their latest name tag, which can be used to good effect in a work environment. For example, qualities such as leadership can be demonstrated by your position as a team captain, committee chairman, playgroup leader and so on.

3. **You are able to complete application forms much quicker**. A large amount of space on application forms is taken up with recording basic facts. If these are already set out in your Personal Data File, it is relatively quick and easy to transfer the details from one to the other,

leaving more time to concentrate on telling the employer why you are applying for the job and what you have to offer.

4. **You will be able to pick out relevant details more quickly when completing other types of application**. A good curriculum vitae (CV) or letter of application is effective only when it concentrates on bringing out *relevant* facts to support your reasons for applying. You will only be able to select these if you have *all* the necessary data in front of you. This is equally important if you are applying for a job by phone.

5. **You can review the image you want to project to employers**. By looking at what you have done in the past and thinking how this can relate to the future, you can focus on your strengths, and highlight any weaknesses which need to be worked on. Above all, you will need to think hard about how to put across anything which you feel puts you in a less than favourable light – such as redundancy, lack of qualifications, or a long break away from the world of work.

SETTING UP YOUR PERSONAL DATA FILE

The main purposes of your file are:

● to set out **facts**
● to identify **skills**.

What you need

Whether you make handwritten notes or use a word-processor, don't be afraid of jotting down rough notes first. Once you are happy that you have all your data, transfer the finished product to A4 sheets, starting a fresh page for each new heading to allow space for updating and revision. Keep the sheets in logical order so you become familiar with where to look for specific pieces of information. When the file is complete, keep it safe in a plastic cover or file to prevent damage through frequent handling.

Keep your Data File together with other documentation – such as certificates, testimonials or records of achievement – in a stiff folder, preferably one with a pocket and flap, to prevent anything becoming lost or misplaced.

Layout

The headings suggested for your file are to help you access information quickly and easily. Some of them may never be used, but it is always better to be prepared; the range of questions asked on some application forms can be quite staggering.

YOUR PERSONAL DETAILS

Name
Record your full name. If you have ever had another name, note this down, together with the date when the change took effect.

Address and telephone number
Note your main home address and telephone number. If you have any other address – such as student lodgings or an alternative address needed for business reasons – record this separately, giving details of when you are likely to be resident there, together with the telephone number for contact purposes.

If you can only be contacted at certain times of day or night on any particular phone number, say when.

Date of birth
For most jobs, your date of birth is all that is required. Make sure you use the following format: 11 April 1967. If you write this date using numbers – 11/4/1967 – this will be misinterpreted as 4 November 1967 if your prospective employer has US connections.

Some application forms ask for your age. Despite pressure on the Government, age discrimination has not been brought into line with other types of discrimination. Employers therefore can still discriminate against you on the grounds of your age. There is in place a Code of Practice – 'Age Diversity in Employment', but this is purely voluntary and you will not be able to take action against an employer who chooses to ignore it.

Other details
You may be asked to provide your National Insurance number or driving licence details. Have these recorded in one place together with any other licence details which might be relevant to your employment.

Place of birth, nationality and family history
There are a whole range of jobs in the Civil Service, the Armed Forces, or any employment connected with the defence industry, where you will be expected to provide not only your place of birth but also details relating to your nationality and that of your parents and spouse. If you have changed your nationality status at any time, note the relevant dates and any additional details which might be required.

Minority status

A growing number of employers operate an equal opportunities policy aimed at increasing the level of representation of minority groups in their work force. To test whether they are reaching the sectors of the working population they want to attract, there are often questions specifically aimed at identifying minority groups – such as the ethnic origin of applicants, the sex, and whether they consider themselves to be disabled. These questions are sometimes attached to a tear-off strip on an application form and the information is removed before the application is considered. However, where a policy of positive discrimination is operating, these questions can appear on the face of the application form itself.

Marital status

Now largely subsumed by the requirement to state your title instead the pros and cons of what to put under this heading will be discussed in greater detail in later chapters. For your own information, however, simply state the facts. Select one of the following:

- Single
- Married
- Separated
- Divorced
- Widowed.

Details of children

Admitting to having children can be the cause of much heart-searching when applying for a job. This topic will be discussed later. In the meantime, simply note down your children's names and dates of birth for reference purposes.

Health

Make a list with dates of any serious illnesses or major surgery you have had. On a separate list note any other aspects of your health which might be the subject of a medical questionnaire. For example:

- Is your sight or hearing impaired, and to what extent? (Do you need to wear spectacles/contact lenses or a hearing aid?)

- Do you suffer from any chronic (long-term) health problem, such as arthritis, asthma, diabetes, bronchitis, back-pain, RSI (repetitive strain injury), or similar, for which you require regular medication or physiotherapy?

● Do you suffer from, or have you suffered from, any mental health problems which require, or required, treatment?

● What is your height/weight?

And finally:

● What is your NHS number?

YOUR EDUCATION AND TRAINING

Secondary schools and qualifications obtained

An astonishing number of application forms still ask for details of your secondary education. What relevance this might have to your application if you are of mature years is probably minimal, but you may as well be prepared for the question anyway.

Please note the word *secondary* in the heading. Employers are not interested in details of your primary schools.

A suggested layout for your data is set out below.

Name of school (and town/city)	From	To	Qualification Gained Level/Subject/Grade/Date

At this stage make sure you know the whereabouts of all your certificates so you can produce them at interview if they are requested.

Listing further education

List under this heading any educational courses taken after leaving school, *providing they led up to an examination with a recognised qualification.* Please note the distinction. These should include any full-time college or university courses, distance learning, part-time or sandwich courses, or courses run as 'evening classes'. Also include any higher degrees or post-graduate courses of study. If it is useful, keep the list of examinations in one subject together, even if you took these over a period of time. For example:

    RSA Typing: Level 1 Distinction (1982)
                    Level 2 Credit (1984)
                    Level 3 Pass (1986)

This section is NOT the place to list evening classes in basketwork, pottery or car maintenance, which belong to the hobbies and leisure pursuits section later. The only exception to this rule is if you have reached a proficiency level which might have some relevance *if you were applying for a job where this skill could be usefully employed.*

What should you do about full-time courses you began, but did not manage to complete – or where you failed an examination?

As this file is for your own use, include *everything*. Add in any factual explanations if these are relevant. You may be able to obscure a failure by careful presentation later.

Use the same layout as for your secondary education.

Name of College *etc* (and town/city)	From	To	Qualification Gained Subject/Level/Date

Check to make sure you have the necessary documents available to prove you possess these qualifications.

Listing professional or occupational qualifications

List these along with when and how they were acquired. Once again, have the necessary documentary evidence on hand to prove your claim.

Listing training courses

This heading is an all-purpose safety net to pick up courses you may have taken which do not fit neatly into other headings. What makes these courses different from those you entered under 'Further Education' is that many will have been of a short duration and did not necessarily involve an examination. If a certificate of competence or a qualification was obtained, make a separate note of this so it does not get forgotten.

Many firms run in-house courses in a wide range of subjects. Some relate specifically to the business of the firm: others are on more general topics such as health and safety, leadership skills, team building or management techniques. If you have attended any such courses, make a note of their title, course content and how long the course lasted. If there was any project you completed as part of the course, give details of this as well.

Include any courses run by your occupational or professional association as part of a career development programme, as well as any courses undertaken because you were interested in the topic – such as first aid, bereavement counselling, communicating with the deaf, navigation techniques, advanced motoring, drama therapy and so on. List the skills you acquired by taking these courses.

SERVICE WITH THE ARMED FORCES

Note the period of service, promotion dates and final rank, and detail any overseas tours.

WORK EXPERIENCE OR CAREER HISTORY

In this section you are not just providing details of previous employers and a string of job titles. You are aiming to identify skills you used or acquired in each job. The suggested layout on page 18 is to provide you with basic headings only. You may well need to allow more space – particularly for 'Key tasks/responsibilities'. Alternatively, you can list these separately.

Begin with your first job, moving forward to the present day: it is much simpler to remember dates this way and you are less likely to leave any unintentional gaps. Remember, however, that you will use this information

EMPLOYMENT RECORD

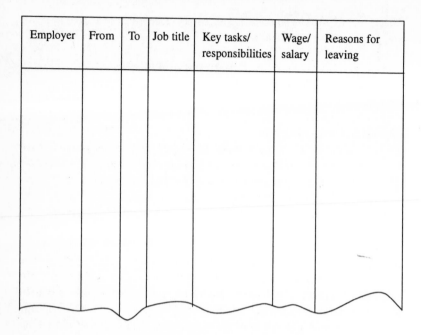

Employer	From	To	Job title	Key tasks/ responsibilities	Wage/ salary	Reasons for leaving

Fig. 1. Your employment record sheet.

in an entirely different way when you come to make your applications. (Any part-time or temporary employment more than ten years ago can be reduced to one-line explanations.)

If you have just left school or college with only short-term employment or limited work experience, note down the relevant details *even though you may use this information in a different way when applying for a job.*

Employers' details

All you need under this heading is the company's name, the location (not the complete address as this takes up too much space), *and the category* which describes the business. This is important if it is not clear from the name of the firm, or the type of work you were engaged in. For instance:

T A Roberts Ltd, Hull   Clerical Assistant Finance Department   Processing invoices to meet payment deadlines

This tells a recruiter absolutely nothing about the line of business T A Roberts Ltd was operating.

Dates employed

Keep this simple. The month and year are enough. If you have some awkward gaps in your employment record, don't be tempted to reduce this date to stating the year only. Some employers ask for the month as well, simply to draw out this very point.

Job title

These are often quite meaningless: you can be a supervisor in charge of three or 30 staff, or an administrative assistant with a small number of duties or a whole range. Nonetheless, job titles are still requested, particularly on application forms, so they need recording.

Your key tasks/responsibilities

This section is all about work-related *skills*. Don't rush it or fill up the space with lists of duties, meaningless phrases, empty jargon or minute detail.

Employers are primarily interested in what you have been doing for the last five years; slightly less interested in what you were doing five years before that; and largely uninterested in what you did any earlier. With this in mind, any jobs which come within the third group can either be lumped together (if they were basically similar), or summed up as one-liners. This becomes essential to reduce the volume of data when completing application forms or CVs. For example:

```
MacKay and Tague, Edinburgh   )
Wm Jackson, Doncaster          )  1970-1976 Labourer
Henry Collins & Son, Dover     )  House building
(Building contractors)
```

This is quite sufficient detail: it shows your experience with all three contractors was on a domestic scale, and did not involve the Channel tunnel or a nuclear power station which would demand very different skills.

When dealing with jobs within the last ten years, a different technique is needed. There are three reasons for this:

1. You want to be clear about the *most important* aspects of the job.

2. You want to be able to show a prospective employer how well you coped with these.

3. You want to use your previous experience to illustrate you have the right skills, aptitudes or qualifications for the job on offer.

An example to study

Maggie Simmons has resigned from her job in a county council home for the elderly because she and her husband have moved to another part of the UK. She is now looking for a new job similar to her old one and wants to emphasise her potential as someone who could be considered for promotion in the future. She lists her key tasks below.

Job Title – Night Care Assistant
Key Tasks:

- To administer medicine and change dressings.

- To contact doctors, social workers and families if a resident was sick.

- To check on residents during the night when there was an alarm call.

- To toilet and bath residents.

- To make hot drinks for suppers.

- To check authorised access to the building.

- To record accidents.

- To help residents wash and dress in the morning.

- To change bedding when necessary.

Maggie's list tells her potential employer nothing at all about what she has to offer now or in the future. Why is this?

1. **It is muddled**. Some of the duties could be better grouped under broader headings, such as health, welfare and security. Others should not be classed as key tasks.

2. **It says nothing about the level of responsibility of the post**. How many other night care assistants were on duty – two, three, or was Maggie on her own?

3. **It gives no indication of the number of residents being cared for or their precise category**. The word 'residents' rather than 'children' supplies a clue that Maggie was responsible for adults. But it is not clear whether these adults were elderly, elderly confused, or younger physically or mentally disabled. This distinction is important to identify the skills Maggie has to offer.

4. **It gives no indication of any personal targets achieved or skills acquired**. Maggie's prospective employer would want to know not just what Maggie was supposed to do in her job but how well she did it and if she is promotion material. Success in service jobs, where there are no sales targets to use as bench marks, can be difficult to illustrate, but not impossible. Extra responsibilities or some other mark of recognition may be available as proof.

In any job application, you should aim to show you have achieved a particular level of competence in previous employment *which can be seen as a positive advantage to your application*. Note down any occasions which would illustrate this so that the information can be used to good effect.

Maggie should have listed her key tasks as set out below.

Job Title – Night Care Assistant

Responsible for:

● Providing care and support where required, to twelve elderly residents between the ages of 81 and 96, including personal help with bathing, toileting and dressing.
● Giving correct medication and changing dressings, as instructed, and informing doctors, family and social workers immediately in cases of urgent treatment.
● Keeping accurate records of accidents and ensuring these were completed as soon as possible, and the Manager informed promptly.
● Keeping a twice-nightly check on the security of the building and anyone wanting to enter or leave it, and helping with any evacuation as set out in the fire safety procedures.
These duties were shared between myself and three other night care assistants.
I also deputised for the Manager on three separate nights during the last three months in emergency situations.

What we now have is a very much rounder picture of Maggie's duties; her working environment; her own perception of her job and the level of responsibility involved. Her skills are also more clearly defined: she is able to follow instructions; can work as part of a team, and is able to manage her time well. Can you identify any others?

Maggie now comes across as someone reliable, competent, and caring who was chosen to act in a deputising role during an emergency on three separate occasions recently. This gives some measure of Maggie's success in her job as well as her potential in the future.

Identifying skills in the workplace

Thinking through your own key tasks, how could you put your perception of those duties into a more interesting context to reveal your skills and level of competence?

Most work activities involve at least two of the following headings:

- people
- money
- products
- ideas.

Study your last job and answer the following six questions under the relevant headings above:

WHO? WHAT? WHEN? WHERE? WHY? HOW?

The following pages set out two possible ways of doing this. Pages 23 and 24 tackle the problem one way; pages 25 and 26 another. Look in particular at the *type of word used* to describe activities under the **WHY**, **WHAT** and **SKILLS** headings. What do you notice about them?

Using whichever format you prefer, set out your own key tasks using the same type of word to describe what you do, or did in your last job, and what skills you needed to do it well.

Once you have completed this exercise, draw together the various aspects of the job into a comprehensive, concise series of brief statements like Maggie's. Bring the job to life, and your personality and skills with it.

KEY TASKS – PEOPLE

WHO do I meet?	The public	Customers/ clients	Subordinates	Colleagues	Bosses
WHEN? eg daily, weekly, monthly	daytime night-time all hours	daytime night-time when required	at set times when required	on duty handovers	on duty
WHERE do I meet them?	on premises at home	on premises at client's premises	on premises elsewhere	on premises elsewhere	on premises elsewhere
WHY do I meet them?	to provide help	to expand business to promote products	to train to develop to maintain morale to supervise	to foster teamwork to maintain team spirit	to evaluate progress to receive guidance
WHAT skills do I use?	advising listening recording	selling purchasing persuading	delegating organising training checking	informing listening co-ordinating	informing listening contributing
HOW do I measure my success	no further queries no complaints satisfaction expressed	customer loyalty broadening of client base increased sales targets reached	good morale low staff turnover better qualified staff	good working relations good team spirit consistency of approach	recognition promotion guidance

Fig. 2. Key tasks dealing with people.

KEY TASKS – MONEY TRANSACTIONS

WHO is involved?	*General public*	*Customers/clients*	*Staff*
WHEN? eg daily, weekly, monthly	weekly fortnightly monthly on demand	monthly on demand within 3 months	weekly monthly when needed
WHERE or how do transactions take place?	on premises at home through banks by post	on premises at client's premises through banks by post over the phone	on premises elsewhere through banks by post

WHY do transactions take place?	to meet needs
	to meet legal
	    requirements
	to dispense aid
	to receive money
		to meet debts
		to raise debts
		to cover debts
			to reward
			    service
			to reimburse
			    expenses
			to cover
			    costs

WHAT skills do I use?	assessing classifying informing checking recording	monitoring calculating informing checking recording	calculating applying rules checking compiling informing

HOW do I measure my success	no complaints
	needs met on time
	no errors
	positive feedback
		prompt payment
		no complaints
		no errors
		willingness of customers
		    to continue business
			no
			    complaints
			payment on
			    time
			no errors

Fig. 3. Key tasks dealing with money.

KEY TASKS – PRODUCTS

WHO are the products made for?
- The market generally?
- One outlet?
- Several?
- Individuals?

WHAT product(s) are made?
- Components?
- Finished articles?

Timescale involved (**WHEN**)?
- X items in Y time?
- Regular deadline?
- On demand?

WHERE does production take place?
- Factory?
- Workshop?
- At home?

Main tasks of your job (**WHY**)?
- To install machines?
- To organise distribution?
- To maintain safety?
- To check quality?
- To co-ordinate shifts?
- To repair machinery?

HOW do you measure success?
- By meeting supply dates?
- By controlling costs?
- By maintaining quality?
- By expanding orders?
- By completing repairs quickly?

SKILLS needed for me to achieve success?
- Technical
- Organising
- Dexterity
- Supervisory
- Delegation
- Operational
- Craft/Artistic

Fig. 4. Key tasks dealing with products.

KEY TASKS – IDEAS

WHO needs the ideas?

- Customers?
- Yourself?
- Colleagues?
- Boss?

WHAT ideas are wanted?

- Artistic?
- Scientific?
- Business?

WHEN are the ideas needed?

- On demand?
- Within a set timescale?

WHERE does production take place?

- At home?
- In a studio?
- In a laboratory?
- Brainstorming sessions?
- Team discussions?

WHY do you create ideas?

- To give pleasure to others?
- To satisfy personal needs?
- To advance science?
- To advance medicine?
- To improve business efficiency?

HOW do you measure success?

- By further commissions?
- By public recognition?
- By meeting deadlines?
- By keeping within budgets?
- By making a breakthrough?

SKILLS needed to achieve success

- Artistic/Creative
- Technical
- Managerial
- Interpretive
- Evaluative

Fig. 5. Key tasks handling ideas.

Reasons for leaving and gaps in employment

Most reasons for leaving an employer are obvious – such as:

I couldn't stand the boss.
I wanted more money.
I got thoroughly fed up with the whole business.
It was a rotten organisation.
I couldn't cope.

But these are not the sort of reasons you can afford to list in an application. You have to think of something *positive* – and believable – which you can justify if you were questioned on the topic more closely in an interview. Possibilities include:

I wanted to vary my experience in . . .
I wanted to work for a larger/smaller organisation so that I could
    develop wider skills/specialise in . . .
I was interested in joining a more dynamic sales force.

Whatever you do, ALWAYS avoid a negative impression. This includes using the words REDUNDANT or EARLY RETIREMENT to explain gaps in your career history. There is a 'deadening' effect which attaches to these words. Look them up in any dictionary and you will see for yourself.

Redundant – superfluous, no longer needed.

Retirement – the act of withdrawing, retreating, receding, leaving
    public office or active life.

Thoroughly depressing descriptions. If you have been made redundant or taken early retirement, pick another way of describing your situation. Avoid using downbeat words or phrases which have all the buoyancy of lead balloons. Instead, try something along the following lines:

● The company was relocated/restructured.
● The business was transferred to another company.
● There was a departmental reorganisation.

This is not to pretend you have not been made redundant, or been given early retirement. It is one way of avoiding emphasising events which can be destructive both to your mental well-being and to your approach to potential employers.

Gaps in your employment history involving prison sentences are always a difficult subject. If the offence took place more than ten years ago, and you are not applying for a sensitive post, you could argue the case for filling the gap with the words – 'Not employed'.

Under the **Rehabilitation of Offenders Act 1974** a criminal conviction is regarded as spent, or used up, after two-and-a-half to ten years, depending on the gravity of the offence and the age of the person when convicted. In other words, you no longer have to declare it. However, there are exceptions to this rule. There are a range of jobs involving working with vulnerable groups such as children, the sick or the elderly, the administration of justice, certain professions and posts involved with national security, where you *will have* to give details of **any** convictions, together with relevant dates, because your appointment will be subject to police enquiries. All jobs where these exceptions apply will involve the completion of application forms which will have a section specifically for this purpose.

A criminal record however is not deleted once convictions become spent and in some cases, depending on the gravity or number of offences, will be retained for periods between 10 years and for life. The **Police Act 1997** contains provisions which will enable registered employers to obtain details of criminal records, but the provisions of this Act are not yet in force.

The Probation Service provides immediate support on your release and can help you with filling out forms or by making the initial approach to a Jobcentre. You can also contact the Service on a voluntary basis to ask for help even if you are no longer under their supervision. It should be emphasised, however, that the Service will not make an application for you, and will never act as a referee. If you need any advice and guidance on this topic, contact the **National Association for the Care and Resettlement of Offenders (NACRO)** or the **APEX Trust** who specialise in promoting employment opportunities for ex-offenders. Both organisations are listed under 'Useful Addresses' on p. 157.

Last wage or salary

This is a question which is still popular, particular with companies who are prepared to negotiate a salary rather than state one. (The morality and reasons for this policy will be considered in Chapter 3.) For the purposes of your Personal Data File simply record the relevant information, setting out the basic wage or salary, with any bonus payments or commission separately.

CURRENT MEMBERSHIP OF ASSOCIATIONS, PUBLIC BODIES *ETC*

This section is to highlight your membership of any professional or occupation-related body, tribunal, board of governors, council or whatever. Set out your details under the following headings and record your main duties if you had any in terms of the skills required to function effectively in your role.

Name of organisation	Year joined	Main duties and any positions held (with dates)

PASTIMES

Hobbies, leisure pursuits and voluntary work

This is one of the areas where if you are a school leaver, a graduate or a woman returner with little work experience, you can provide evidence of transferable or portable skills, *ie* skills which can be shaped or redirected into job skills.

Don't lump these three aspects of your spare time activities into one category without a second thought: they are very different and need to be treated separately. Why? For the following reasons:

- **Hobbies** – are activities you do yourself.

- **Leisure pursuits** – are activities you watch other people do.

- **Voluntary work** – are activities you do for other people.

Looked at in this way, you can see they are quite distinct. You can also see that your pastimes tell someone quite a lot about the sort of person you are:

a loner or part of a team; a doer or a watcher; a carer or an individualist. Similarly, if you had any particular role in a more formally structured group, such as secretary, treasurer, chairman, team captain *etc*, this too can be a useful signal to an employer. So take the trouble to identify aspects of your pastimes *which could be related to the world of work.*

Be on the look-out for any skills which are needed. Identify at least three for each. For example:

- sewing
  - – ability to follow instructions
  - – manual dexterity
  - – good hand/eye co-ordination

- football player
  - – ability to work as part of a team
  - – quick response time
  - – ability to follow instructions

- recording tapes for the blind
  - – literacy
  - – clear speaking voice
  - – ability to use recording equipment

When completing your list using the suggested table on page 31, include only those pastimes which you are *currently involved in or which you have only given up recently but intend to restart.* Don't include anything you do only on an occasional basis, either to pad out your data, or to impress. You could find yourself out of your depth at an interview trying to answer probing questions on a topic you have lost touch with.

LISTING YOUR EVERYDAY SKILLS

We all have skills we tend to take for granted because they are not primarily used or associated with the world of work. If you have any additional skills, note them down. Some, if not all, could be portable. Here are some possibilities:

- driving
- languages
- other communication skills
- keyboard/information technology skills
- caring or catering.

Driving

Some jobs depend on the applicant being mobile. If you can drive, note

PASTIMES/SKILLS

Hobbies

Organisation	Dates	Details (and any positions held)	Skills involved (list at least three for each)

Leisure pursuits

Organisation	Dates	Details	Any skills involved

Voluntary work

Organisation	Dates	Details (and any positions held)	Skills involved (list at least three for each)

Fig. 6. Your record of pastimes and the skills you use.

down the type of licence you hold, how long you have held it, and any endorsements you may have. If you have passed the Advanced Driving Test or taken Pass Plus, note these down too.

Languages

You may not have had any formal training in a particular language but you may belong to a bi-lingual or even a multi-lingual family or community. If you are *fluent* in any language through usage, this is often more valuable to an employer than fluency through study.

Other communication skills

Can you use sign language to communicate with deaf people? Do you know how to lip-speak properly? Can you understand braille? What about semaphore?

Keyboard/technology skills

Don't forget any keyboard skills you acquired in the dim and distant past and never thought you would use again. These can always be resurrected with a little practice and now is as good a time as any.

Similarly you may have had a temporary or holiday job which involved using computerised tills or stock-checks, accounts or records; you may have had experience in modern printing methods or computer aided design. You may have spent some time homeworking or teleworking using the Internet and fax machines, or a word-processor.

In an increasingly technological world of work, anything which shows you have some grasp of the changes which have taken place over the last few years, or could demonstrate that you have the ability to transfer older skills into the new environment, should be given pride of place.

Caring or catering

Skills acquired in bringing up a large family, nursing sick children or elderly relatives, tend to be taken for granted, but they are skills nonetheless. The experience may also have given you a greater maturity and understanding of certain disabilities or illnesses which you could pass on to others.

The term 'housewife' still tends to carry with it the assumption that women who have spent several years looking after a family and then want to return to work have no experience to offer. This is simply not true.

There will obviously be differences in the level of experience and responsibility – as there are in any paid job. Looking after one child is less demanding than two or three. Managing on a large budget is easier than a small one. Cleaning a small house is less demanding than a large one, and so on. But the basic need to manage priorities and time are common to all.

Here are some of the skills associated with the successful running of a home and family:

- Budgeting
- Time management
- Forward planning
- Stock control and re-ordering
- Maintenance
- Catering
- Diplomacy/negotiating skills
- Training/teaching

This is not an exhaustive list, but only a brief summary to set your mind thinking along these lines. What other skills could be added to this list?

No one would pretend every housewife excels at everything, just as no one in any other line of work excels at the whole range of duties they undertake. But if you are a housewife and you manage your job well, you are basically completing tasks normally associated with management in the workplace. Don't forget this and don't down-grade your abilities or self-image because of old prejudices or ignorance on the part of others.

GIVING REFERENCES

Make a note of at least two people's names and addresses who would act as referees if required. Preferably, these should be work-related. Expect your present or your immediate past employer to be approached as well.

Referees should know you intend to put their names forward and it is also up to you to keep them informed on how your job-hunting is progressing. You should also keep them up-to-date with any relevant information, such as additional training courses you attend, new qualifications achieved, voluntary work involvement, and so on.

References which contain observations such as

'I am not sure what area of work Miss Hamilton has been employed in since leaving my company . . .' or

'I am unable to say whether Mr Jordan would be suitable for this post . . .'

will do your cause more harm than good.

Occasionally, you are also asked to provide one referee who will testify to your good character. Be sensible about this. Pick someone who has sufficient status who also knows you well enough, not just a close friend or acquaintance.

USING YOUR PERSONAL DATA FILE

When you have completed your file it should contain everything you need to know about yourself.

Your file should also be a dynamic and not static piece of work. You must take the time to review its contents on a regular basis; you should update anything which needs revision; and you should remind yourself frequently of all the qualities and skills you have to offer. The more you put into your file, the better it will work for you.

YOUR JOB RECORD FILE

The purpose of this file is to provide you with a safe haven for all the relevant papers you may have for every application, including:

● the job advertisement
● any documents relating to the job or the organisation offering it (job description, company reports, organisational framework, relevant data from your own research)
● copies of the application letter, application form or CV
● any additional correspondence
● notes on 'on spec' visits
● notes on telephone conversations.

You may prefer to have a separate folder for each job to make absolutely sure you can identify what you want at a glance, or a simple colour-coded range of dividers in a ring binder. Whatever you choose it should be easy to use and should keep the documentation in good condition. Remember you may need to take some of the documents with you to an interview at a later date.

The Progress Sheet

Regardless of what form your Job Record File takes, draw up a Progress Sheet to keep at the front along the lines suggested opposite. In this way, you have an immediate at-a-glance record of what stage each application has reached (see Figure 7).

If you have several irons in the fire at the same time, you need to keep an eye on progress. Some of them may need reheating – should you have

Job Title and name of firm	Details		Application		Interview	
	Sent for	Rec'd	Made	Ack'd	Date	Result
1.						
2.						
3.						
4.						

Fig. 7. Job applications Progress Sheet.

received an acknowledgement by now? Others might have reached the stage of having to be pulled out and discarded – has the date passed when you were told to expect to hear something?

Don't let the opportunity of a job slip through your fingers for the want of a little effort.

SUMMING UP

There has been a lot to think about in this chapter – and perhaps rather more than you expected. If you have completed all your groundwork properly, you should now be more aware of the range of skills you have to offer.

Increasingly, employers are looking for evidence of skills, or the presence of portable skills, not just qualifications. Qualifications are simply the basic requirement all applicants are expected to have. What you must try to do is to make your application the one which stands out from the rest. Make it interesting. Give it a sparkle which attracts attention. Make it say – Here is someone worth seeing.

ACTION CHECKLIST

● Be thorough in collating personal details and documentation for your Personal Data File.

● Keep educational certificates, professional diplomas etc with your Personal Data documents for easy reference.

● Check your employment history is fully recorded.

● Identify the skills you have used or developed during previous employment or through outside work activities.

● Keep your referees up-to-date with any changes in your life or employment history.

● Update your Personal Data File as soon as any changes occur.

● Review your Job Record File Progress Sheet on a regular basis.

● Keep all documents in a safe place.

2

Planning Your Strategy

KNOWING WHAT YOU WANT

Knowing who you are and what you have to offer is only part of the job search. The other side of the coin is knowing what you are looking for.

One of the main problems facing anyone in the jobs market, particularly anyone under pressure to find employment, is targeting the right job. It is all too easy to persuade yourself to adopt the 'scattergun' approach – that is, firing off at everything and anything in the hope of hitting something. You might, but equally well you might not, which is wasteful of your time and energy – and very dispiriting.

Your job search strategy *must* include knowing precisely what you are aiming for and why. To do this you must identify what you believe to be the perfect job for you and to keep this 'image of perfection' as the main goal. Circumstances may force you to modify your ideal, but the main characteristics should still be there. These are what will make the difference between having a job which gives you a sense of satisfaction, and having a job which makes your working life a misery.

You might be certain about the type of employment you are seeking – salesman, secretary, town planner, mechanic – but you also need to know:

- the working environment which suits you best
- the level of work most appropriate to your skills
- the minimum financial return necessary
- the geographical location in which you want to work.

Think these headings through thoroughly and jot down what conclusions you come to. These notes can then be kept either in your Personal Data File or as part of your Job Record File, but they must be kept: they are to remind you of what you are aiming for and to prevent you from straying back to the scattergun approach.

At the end of the chapter (page 48) is a suggested format to put together a comprehensive list of your findings.

THE WORKING ENVIRONMENT

Which working environment suits you best? You may be quite definite about what this is, either because your previous jobs have been in broadly similar environments, or because the majority of your working life has been with one employer.

But if you have doubts, or if you have never had a job, or if you are returning to work after a career break of several years, how do you know what sort of working environment is right for you? Which do you prefer?

- indoors/outdoors
- static/mobile
- solitary/in a group
- in the front line/behind the scenes
- with your peer group/with a mixed age range
- working with people/animals/products/money?

Your working environment is important: you are going to spend the majority of your waking hours in it, so it must be right, or as near to right as possible, otherwise you can suffer from stress.

If you have always worked in the same environment is this what you want in future – or would you feel more comfortable in a different situation?

Incidentally, changing your working environment has nothing to do with changing your career. This is quite a separate issue which is outside the scope of this book. In changing your working environment you are not changing *what* you do, but *how* you do it.

If you have no work experience to help you decide which working environment is best for you, or if you are having second thoughts, a few moments studying your list of pastimes will give you a good indication. Remember pastimes are what you choose to do, not what someone tells you to do, so they are excellent pointers to the type of situations you prefer.

You may find you have strong preferences – all your pastimes being either solitary or team activities – or you may have a mixture of both which gives you greater flexibility.

From what you have discovered about your preferred environment, decide which of the working conditions you *must* have and which you would prefer to have but could be a bit flexible about. Then fill out the relevant section at the end of the chapter for future reference.

CHOOSING THE RIGHT LEVEL OF WORK

Here you are considering what level of work you need to match your skills and abilities. Thinking about this is basically a matter of common sense and not getting carried away by flights of fancy.

If you are a school leaver, for example, you are more likely to be successful if you look for a junior post, where previous work experience is not expected, or at least is less likely to play a major part in your selection. You are wasting your time applying for jobs which require a higher level of experience or skills. The job might sound very attractive, but you are trying to run before you can walk.

If you have been away from paid employment for several years, you may also find it easier to get a job where you work as part of a team, or under supervision, until you find your feet. This does not apply of course if you have been playing a leading role in the community or in a voluntary association, with duties and responsibilities which could be directly transferred into the working environment.

If you have been made redundant or given early retirement, you may not want to look for a job with the same level of responsibility as before; or perhaps you are determined not to lose status; or even dead set on the next step up the ladder. (The same could also be said of anyone who simply wants to change their job.) Regardless of the motivation which drives you, you must look at your last job critically and put it into context with others on the market. Comparisons between jobs can be very difficult, not least because job titles can be so misleading.

Set out on page 40 is a questionnaire to help you. After the title, describe the status you would give the job such as:

- junior/trainee/apprentice
- qualified/time-served
- supervisory
- junior management
- middle management
- senior management
- professional

and think what this represents in terms of your responsibilities, and how the post fitted into the rest of the organisation. Did the job title match up to the duties, or was it an artificial tag which hid the unvarnished truth? The following are just some examples of the misuse of job titles for jobs which are basically routine:

administrative assistant	=	clerk
office manager	=	general dogsbody
finance officer	=	bookkeeper

LEVEL OF LAST JOB

Job Title: ....

Status: ....

How many others in the firm had the same/similar job title?.........................

Did you have to report to anyone or be supervised by them?   YES/NO

Were you happy with this situation?   YES/NO

If NO, why not?..

....

Did anyone have to report to you or be supervised by you?   YES/NO

If YES, how many people were involved ....

Were you happy with this situation?   YES/NO

If NO, why not?..

....

Does status matter to you?   YES/NO

If YES, does the job title matter more than job content?   YES/NO

Do you believe your job title reflected your true status?   YES/NO

If NO, what do you believe your job title should have been? ....

....

In your last job how well did you cope?   Well/adequately/badly

Did this affect your reason for leaving?   YES/NO

If YES, in what way? ....

Do you believe this might affect the level of your next job?   YES/NO

If YES, in what way? ....

In your next job do you want less/the same/more responsibility?

What reasons do you have to support this?......................................

Fig. 8. Assessing the level of your last job.

secretary	=	audio-typist
works manager	=	time-keeper/wages clerk

If you start looking through situations vacant columns with the wrong idea about the level of job you are searching for, this can lead to innumerable fruitless applications – and a lot of frustration. Stop thinking in terms of job titles and more in terms of job content. Studying the list of key tasks and responsibilities you identified in your Personal Data File will help to clarify this.

Just as you must not make the mistake of overselling yourself, you must not undersell yourself either. Job titles can not only inflate the status of a job, they can deflate it as well. For example:

administrative assistant	=	committee administrator
office manager/works manager	=	personnel officer/industrial relations officer
finance officer	=	financial adviser
secretary	=	personal assistant

Here are situations where higher levels of skills and experience are required than suggested by the descriptive titles. Look beyond the job title to the job itself and recognise it for what it really is then complete the section at the end of the chapter under the appropriate heading.

WEIGHING UP THE FINANCIAL RETURN

For most people what the job pays is the most crucial factor. Unfortunately this can sometimes cloud your judgement about the job and your suitability for it.

If you have just left school or college, you may feel justifiably proud of your educational achievements and be tempted to look around for jobs which match this sense of pride. But educational qualifications alone are a poor guide to what you can offer as an employee. The world of work is light-years away from the world of school or college, so until you have some experience under your belt and broadened your range of skills, don't expect an employer to offer you a fortune.

Similarly, if you are returning to work after a career break, you may have to accept the fact that you will not attract as high a wage or salary as others in your age group until, or unless, you can prove that your experience and skills match those of others who have not made the break.

If you are out of work and have a family to support, the pressures to succeed in the job market are intense. *Any job is better than no job* – if you like. Faced with this situation, make sure this move is the last option on your list – not the first, or you could jeopardise your future prospects.

Crucially, if you are the breadwinner in your family, you must be certain of how much you need to earn to meet basic living costs. A job which does not meet even your basic minimum means you literally cannot afford to work.

Set out on pages 44 and 45 is a list of possible weekly/monthly living expenses. Use either weekly or monthly averages as a basis for comparing potential earnings with potential outgoings. Add your various bills together for the last full year and divide them either by 52 for weekly costs, or by 12 to obtain a monthly equivalent. When you have calculated the grand total of the first column, you know how much you have to earn *in order to keep your existing standard of living*.

Go through the list again. Ask yourself if you could cut back on any *non-essential items*. Be realistic. Don't make false economies like cutting out the house insurance or costs of general repairs and maintenance. Magazines, tobacco and entertainment are the most obvious headings to cut first. Your partner's allowance and children's pocket money are important, but if times get really tough and it takes you longer to find a job than you expected, it may be necessary to reduce these amounts too. Before matters reach this stage, however, start discussing this openly and honestly with your family. You are going to need their support and they will need to understand why it may not be possible to continue with their accustomed lifestyle.

Note your revised figures in the second column and add these together. The grand total represents *the minimum wage or salary you can consider*. Going any lower will put you and your family in real financial difficulties.

When you have completed this exercise, put your findings under the relevant headings on page 48 at the end of the chapter.

DECIDING THE LOCATION

Right from the start you must have some ideas about the geographical location of your job search. However, you must also be prepared to consider other possibilities if time passes and you are not having any success. This is particularly important in an area where there is higher than average unemployment, or your skills and experience are in competition with thousands of others.

Geographical locations can be:

- locally (within easy walking distance)
- within commuting distance (anything over about three miles)
- in other areas (too far to commute).

Local employment

Much depends on where you live. Towns or cities not dependent on one particular industry may have a wide choice of jobs available and a broad range of salaries on offer. An urban area suffering from a downturn in its general economy, however, presents a different picture. Demand for work is likely to exceed supply, there is less on offer, and what is available may be less well paid.

In rural locations, local jobs are much thinner on the ground, and are usually less well-paid for the same reason. There are also other factors such as seasonal fluctuations associated with agriculture or tourism, and the consequent heavy reliance on temporary or part-time work. There is also the problem of finding a job which will lead on naturally to better pay and prospects.

Commuting

Commuting is only worthwhile if you do not spend too much time and money on travel. This means there are several aspects to consider:

- financial implications
- personal commitments
- mode of transport.

Irrespective of whether or not you are an independent free spirit or someone with a family to support, if you intend to commute when you have not done so previously, remember to include the revised cost of travel when weighing up the financial returns of various jobs on offer.

Your personal commitments are just as important, particularly if commuting means losing large slices of your existing free time. You can afford to drop your role as a member of a darts team, but family commitments are another matter, especially if you currently play a major role in child-care arrangements early or late in the day. You cannot expect your partner to simply drop his or her employment to fit into your new arrangements – particularly if their job prospects are better, or are likely to be more stable, than your own. Childminders or nannies can be an expensive alternative and suitable or well-qualified personnel are not that easy to find.

How you intend to commute is also important. Would you have to drive or take the train/bus? What would this mean in terms of your physical well-being at the end of a day? What effect would this have on your home life? Is this acceptable?

These are not questions you should brush aside. They are often crucial to the survival of the family unit. Your family may need the income you earn, but they may need your presence more.

WEEKLY/MONTHLY EXPENDITURE

		Present £	Revised £
House	Mortgage/rent		
	Building insurance		
	Contents insurance		
	Council tax		
	Water rates		
	Electricity		
	Gas		
	Telephone		
	TV rental/licence		
	Maintenance		
	Replacements	_____	_____
		_____	_____
Housekeeping	Basic food		
	Drink		
	Cleaning		
	Laundry	_____	_____
		_____	_____
Travel	Car loan repayments		
	Tax/insurance		
	Maintenance		
	MOT		
	Petrol		
	Train fares		
	Bus fares		
	Hire charges	_____	_____
		_____	_____
Family costs	Schooling expenses		
	Clothing (children)		
	Partner's allowance		
	Children's pocket money		
	Outstanding loans (list)		
	....		
	....		
	Additional expenses (list)		
	....	_____	_____
		_____	_____

Fig. 9. Your weekly/monthly budget for personal expenditure.

		Present £	Revised £
Personal items	Insurance premiums		
	....		
	....		
	....		
	Subscriptions (list)		
	....		
	....		
	....		
	Maintenance to former spouse/children		
	Savings schemes		
	Toiletries		
	Medicine		
	Dental charges		
	Clothes		
	Tobacco		
	Newspapers/magazines		
	Entertainment		
	Recreational/holiday costs		
	Birthday/Christmas expenses		
	Pocket money		
	Extra (specify)		
	....		
	....	———	———
Add in 10% for cost of living increases and unforeseen expenses			
GRAND TOTAL		———	———

Deciding on relocation

Should you move to another area? If you are independent this is very much a viable option.

If you have never worked away from home, however, go through the financial exercise on page 44. Get someone with experience of calculating living expenses to help you put some figures together. They will of necessity have to be rough and ready, but they will at least give you some idea of the costs involved and the need to take these into account if you are having to meet all the expenses from your own pocket.

If you have dependants, maybe a house to sell and children of school age, relocation can become a nightmare. The following are only some of the questions you will need to consider.

1. Selling the house
How long can you expect your property to be on the market before it sells? What figure can you expect to get for your house? Are properties in the area you are hoping to move to less expensive/more expensive/about the same? What will be the total cost of removal, including solicitors' fees, stamp duty, search fees, removal firm charges, new carpets/curtains, decorating *etc*? Can you afford to pay two mortgages if your old property does not sell?

2. Finding your partner a new job
What job vacancies would be available in the new area which would be suitable? Would moving damage your partner's career? Is there likely to be a drop in expected income? What effect would this have on the family? What would happen if your partner could not get a job?

3. Your children's schooling
Are there suitable schools in the new area to meet your children's needs? Are your children reaching a crucial stage in their education where a move might be detrimental to their progress? Does the education authority compare favourably with your existing one or not? What additional financial costs will you incur by moving your children?

4. Other dependants
Is there an ageing parent who relies on your physical help? Would you have to consider moving him or her with you? What would be the implications of doing this? (Depending on individual circumstances, these could be very far reaching indeed.) What alternatives are open to you?

All the above points make the assumption that the family unit is prepared to agree to relocating in the first place. Don't assume this. If you are really intent on looking for a job well outside your immediate geographical area, you must talk through your ideas with those who will be directly affected by your decision. You cannot afford to take them for granted. You must not impose your wishes on them, particularly if you are acting out of impulse rather than sound judgement. You really have to listen and answer their concerns. To be successful, you are going to need more than their grudging support. Your partner might not be willing to give up his or her job. Your children's education and consequently their own employment prospects in future could be placed in jeopardy. An elderly relative may simply not be strong enough to make the move with you and faces an uncertain future.

The stresses of moving house and starting a new job at the same time should not be taken on board lightly. You do not want to add to your load by dragging in your wake a partner and children who feel resentful or angry, or an ageing parent left behind isolated and lonely. Too many families break up today. Don't let yours become one of these sad statistics.

When you have given serious thought to where you intend to concentrate your job search, fill in the appropriate details on page 48 together with any additional information.

YOUR PERFECT JOB

You should now have a rough sketch of what you want most from a job. This is your 'ideal'.

This does not mean you will necessarily find the perfect match – in fact, this is extremely unlikely – but at least you have something to guide you on your way. You can change this ideal at any time, but what you change must be limited to those factors where you are able to be flexible. Do NOT change any aspects you firmly believe you *must* have. These are your foundation stones. If you have given this exercise enough thought, you should have no grounds for shifting them.

ACTION CHECKLIST

● Identify your ideal working environment.

● Identify the level of responsibility you know is right for you.

● Calculate the minimum financial return you need to meet your commitments.

● Be certain about the best geographical location for your job search.

● Make sure any dependants agree with your decisions on finance and job location.

MY PERFECT JOB

Working environment

    What I must have   ....
    (and why)   ....
                       ....

    Other conditions I would   ....
    prefer (and why)   ....
                       ....
                       ....

Level of work

    Level I want to have   ....
    (give details)   ....

    Level I would be   ....
    prepared to accept   ....
    (give details)   ....

Financial return

    Wage or salary I want   ....
    (not including bonus   ....
    payments, commission *etc*) ....

    The minimum wage or   ....
    salary I can afford   ....

Location

    Where I want to work   ....
    (and why)   ....
    Second choice   ....
    (and why)   ....
    Where I would work   ....
    as a last resort   ....
    (and why)   ....

Fig. 10. Use this questionnaire to describe your perfect job.

3

Starting Your Job Search

SOURCES OF INSPIRATION

Now you know what you have to offer an employer and what you see as your ideal job, this is the point where your job search really begins.

Just to re-cap for a moment, remember your primary aim now is to reduce wastage of energy, time and money in futile applications. There are no prizes handed out for completing 50 or more applications a week – especially if you don't land a single interview for all your effort. Instead you should be concentrating your search in the corner of the job market which will produce the best results for your efforts. This will depend on what you are looking for, but the most likely sources of inspiration are:

- careers service providers
- Jobcentres
- shop windows/notice boards
- recruitment agencies
- local newspapers
- national daily newspapers
- trade/professional journals
- libraries
- Internet
- personal contacts.

Using careers service providers

Originally, the careers service only provided help to young people, but over the years this gradually expanded to include other categories of job-seekers. The service has now been taken out of local authority control. Service providers may be listed under a recognisable name in the business section of *The Phone Book*, or under the heading 'Careers Advice' in *The Yellow Pages*. If you are uncertain about what to do, contact your nearest Jobcentre which is listed under 'Employment Service' in the telephone directory.

Using Jobcentres

Jobcentres are able to provide details of jobs available locally and a smaller selection of jobs on offer elsewhere.

The majority of jobs advertised in Jobcentres tend to be either in the lower wage bracket, or on a temporary or casual basis. Employers using Jobcentres are usually keen to have someone start right away, and Jobcentre staff will be happy to make contact with them on your behalf and arrange an interview for you – sometimes immediately.

Using shop windows/notice boards

Some employers wanting locally based employees prefer to advertise vacancies in local shops or on the notice boards in supermarkets. The type of job on offer is likely to be of a fairly basic nature – such as occasional childminding, gardening, or odd-jobbing. Usually the wage offered is quite low.

Some supermarkets, however, use their own notice boards to advertise their own vacancies, ranging from checkout assistants to junior management posts. A whole range of jobs can be on offer if a new store is being opened shortly in the vicinity.

Recruitment agencies

These agencies usually advertise in the press and in *The Yellow Pages*, although several now have their own Web sites on the Internet. They operate by finding suitable staff for clients from a pool of people available for work who are 'on their books'. Their clients pay them fees when a satisfactory placement is made, so they are always on the lookout for new people. There are many smaller agencies which operate at a local level, but there are a few like *Alfred Marks* and *Brook Street* who are very well known. There are also agencies who aim at a specific group of job-hunters, such as senior executives, or those in particular professions.

If you are interested in using their services, discuss what is expected of you first as well as what you can expect from them *before* committing yourself. If you intend to make contact in person, then treat this as you would any interview (which it is), and dress accordingly.

A word of caution here. Some employment agencies are asking applicants to pay a registration fee. *The Employment Agencies Act 1973* makes this practice illegal, except in certain cases – such as the entertainment or fashion model business. If you find yourself being asked to pay a registration fee for agency services, the Department of Trade and Industry (DTI) will want to know. You should contact your nearest Jobcentre or the Employment Agency Standards Office at the address on page 157. Phone calls are charged at local rate.

Internet agencies

Of the agencies who operate solely on the Internet, the most popular are probably *Stepstone.co.uk* and *Monster.co.uk* who have thousands of jobs posted on their jobs boards. These and other reputable sites open up a huge range of job opportunities but this method of recruitment is still in its infancy in the UK and there are areas of concern over the way some sites are operating and over the security of data provided to them. Some sites have been breaching confidentiality, fabricating vacancies to inflate their credibility and copying job advertisements without authorisation from the recruitment source.

There are also other problems. At the moment, if you intend to browse through agency sites you would be wise to do so on stations outside the workplace. This is because when you access a web site, you leave an electronic 'footprint' which can be traced. Programs aptly named 'spiders' have been developed which are being used by less than scrupulous agencies. These programs are designed to crawl through the Net picking up useful CV data from other sites. This is then analysed and acted on. As a result they can feed you job information lifted from other sources which you neither wanted nor asked for; or they can post your CV to employers you did not want to contact, including your own. In some cases, staff wanting to change jobs without their current employer knowing they were actively seeking employment elsewhere have been embarrassed by just such an occurrence.

Both these areas of concern are being investigated by the Department of Trade and Industry with a view to updating the Employment Agencies Act. However, you should remember that the Act will still only cover UK agencies, not those based elsewhere in the world.

Jobsearch sites

There has been a mixed response to the effectiveness of services offered on these sites ranging from being deluged with inappropriate vacancies to the complete reverse of no responses at all. This may be down to poor quality analysis programs or too much information in CVs. In these circumstances terminology you use is triggering an apparent interest or aptitude which might be peripheral in your case rather than the main focus of your job search.

Local newspapers

Local papers offer a wide variety of opportunities from the humble to the exalted. You will find examples of these on pages 62 and 63.

If you are living outside the area of your job search, it pays to get several copies of the local paper not only to give you some idea of the range of employment available and levels of pay on offer, but also house prices, local issues under discussion and so on. Notice how many advertisements offer help with relocation expenses. This may give you some idea of whether employers are confident of getting a local person to fill the vacancy, or are prepared to bring in outside expertise.

National daily newspapers

Jobs on offer here cover not only anywhere in the UK but also abroad. Advertising in the national papers is expensive, so companies using this method are looking for a wide choice of good candidates. The number of recruitment advertisements now offering access to Internet web sites is increasing rapidly and looks like doubling by 2001.

If you are interested in particular categories of employment, some papers advertise these on different days. Newspapers are no longer cheap. If you are counting the pennies, get to know which days are relevant as far as you are concerned by combing the copies held in your local library. You can then decide which days to buy, or on which days to combine a shopping trip with another visit to the library. You can of course contact the editorial office of the paper direct for this information and you will also find job vacancies listed on their web sites.

Trade or professional journals

If you are looking for a job in a particular trade or profession which has its own journal, this is an obvious and important source of job vacancies. These journals also give you a good idea of the comparative wages or salaries being offered for the type of job you are looking for. This may be useful information if you find yourself having to negotiate a salary with a potential employer.

Using libraries

These are excellent sources of information if you intend to make speculative approaches to some employers and want to know more about their businesses.

The Kompass Register lists nearly 30,000 companies in the UK in four volumes, giving such details as office hours, number of employees, product groups, application of products, sales offices, agents and subsidiary companies, as well as a breakdown of each company's financial performance. If you want to know more about a company's international connections, these can be discovered by looking through the *Who Owns Whom* volumes published by Dun and Bradstreet.

Another thick volume is *Kelly's Business Directory* which gives details of manufacturers, wholesalers and suppliers of industrial and professional services throughout the UK. There are around 82,000 companies listed in it, classified under 15,000 trade headings.

Internet

Don't be fooled into thinking the Internet is used only by companies offering jobs with hi-tec or IT content. These certainly predominate at the moment, but there are other opportunities available outside the world of information technology which you might not expect to find – for example, teaching posts at both primary and secondary level, vacancies for statisticians, personnel officers, sales reps, marketing managers, accountants and animal health researchers – even volunteers for charity organisations. It is estimated that by 2001, more than half of all employers in the UK will be using the Internet for recruitment advertising.

Some Web sites merely repeat what you have already read in the newspaper recruitment advert; others provide an in-depth analysis not only of the job on offer, but also the company, its products and its operational size. Others are now using the Net for on-line applications, although the emphasis tends to be on graduate recruitment at the moment. Big names such as Corus, Lloyds TSB and Shell are examples adopting this format.

Where you can apply on-line, you may have the option of completing a standard application form using a personalised password to protect your data, or be asked to post your CV electronically. Alternatively, where the web site is restricted to providing information only, you may be asked to e-mail your application.

Like all new ideas, there have been some teething problems. Some organisations have adopted on-line recruitment without taking on board the need to put in place good standards of service to applicants. There have been complaints of a lack of feed-back which has left some applicants not knowing whether their applications have been received and no indication of when they can assume they have been unsuccessful. Clearly these criticisms have been recognised by some recruiters who are specifying that all applications received at their web site will be acknowledged and applicants kept informed.

Once you know how to log on to the web, it is no more complicated than using a telephone. If you are not on-line at home there are an increasing number of access points where Internet facilities are available, from Internet Cafes to school or college IT departments, where you can learn to browse relevant sites as one more source available to you in your job search.

Personal contacts

Don't discount your network of friends, colleagues or acquaintances who might be able to provide you with useful employment information. This is not to say you should abuse their friendship by expecting them to give you easy access to available jobs if they are in a position to do so; or by expecting them to divulge confidential business information. There is no harm, however, in finding out more about the structure of an organisation, its philosophy, products or services, and making general enquiries about the best way to make an approach, or who to write to or telephone in the first instance.

READING JOB ADVERTISEMENTS

Nothing is ever straightforward in life and job advertisements are no exception. They can tell you everything, or nothing; they can set out absolute requirements, or imply there is room for manoeuvre; they can 'hype' a job almost out of recognition, or hide it beneath a mass of irrelevant jargon; they can be honest attempts to give a true picture of the job on offer, or downright fabrications.

Reading between the lines

Towards the end of this chapter there is a selection of adverts to look at and analyse. In the meantime, to get you into the right frame of mind for this exercise, here are a number of points to think about.

The first thing to remember is DON'T SCAN. This is particularly important where you are faced with a page of closely packed job vacancy columns in a newspaper. Almost automatically after a while your eyes start to drift over the bulk of the printed page without stopping for closer inspection. There are all sorts of reasons why this happens:

- a job title doesn't grab you as being interesting
- an occupational heading doesn't seem relevant
- a single word or phrase gives off negative vibrations

If you don't stop yourself from scanning, you can lose the opportunity of finding a job.

POINTS TO WATCH

Style and layout

The way an advert is presented can tell you a lot about the organisation behind it. It has been mentioned earlier that advertising space, particularly in the national dailies, is expensive: the larger the advert, the greater the cost, so you would expect the more prestigious companies to take up more column inches than smaller ones.

But there is more to an advert than its size. Is there an e-mail or Web site address? What does this tell you about the organisation? How is the advert written? This tells you whether you are dealing with an organisation which prefers to operate on a formal, perhaps even impersonal basis, rather than in a more relaxed fashion. If you are asked to write to an unnamed Personnel Officer, or a Mr Carter, rather than telephone Tina Morris for a chat, you can get a good idea which organisational system the company is operating.

Confusing job titles
Job titles, as you already know from the previous chapter, can be totally misleading.

A Production Assistant to one company can be a Technical Adviser to another and an Assistant Works Manager to a third. The term 'manager' itself covers a wide range of skills and expertise, from junior to senior levels in anything from distribution to marketing, office administration to accountancy.

Just as you did with your own job in Chapter 1, look at job content rather than descriptive titles.

Classification headings
If you are not careful, you can discount whole columns of job vacancies because they have been entered under unexpected or unfamiliar headings. In some cases, the job title itself has been misleading and not every job description fits snugly into the classifications adopted by the various recruitment advertisers. There is also the additional problem of classifications used by one paper not being the same as another.

In-vogue classifications
You need to keep yourself up-to-date with the latest trends in job classifications. For instance, positions once found under 'Training' or 'Personnel' are now often lumped together under the heading 'Human Resource Management'.

If you don't pay attention to the shifting jargon describing your particular line of work, you may miss out on job vacancies which adopt the current in-vogue descriptions. You may feel some of these titles are pretentious, pompous or just downright silly, but you can't afford to ignore them.

Off-putting key words or phrases
Don't be too ready to discard a job because particular words or phrases leap out at you with requirements such as

degree . . .
knowledge of . . .
aged between . . .
qualified in . . .
. . . years' experience

If these words don't give you an immediate positive buzz, you may be tempted to move on to the next advert without a second thought. However, in a surprisingly large number of adverts, these key words or phrases are qualified, or softened. What appears at first glance to be a barrier to your application might not exist, so look out for qualifying words or phrases such as

... would be useful

equivalent to ...

... or similar

... is preferable.

Here an employer has an ideal applicant in mind, but is prepared to accept the fact that flexibility might provide a greater choice of candidates.

There are occasions of course when the employer is not prepared to consider any flexibility at all. Phrases to watch for here are

must be ...

not less than ...

... are essential

... are the minimum expected.

If you do not match up to these absolute requirements but you decide to apply anyway, you must be prepared for failure to make the short-list even if you feel you have made out a good case for being considered because of truly exceptional circumstances.

Ageism

Unlike discrimination on the grounds of race, colour or sex, which is illegal in recruitment, you can be discriminated against quite openly on the grounds of your age. **The Chartered Institute of Personnel and Development (CIPD)** has campaigned for many years for the removal of age limits in job advertisements. The Institute's own publication *People Management* no longer accepts any recruitment advertising which excludes some applicants purely on the grounds of their age. Despite pressure during the late '90s to bring age discrimination into line with other areas of unlawful discrimination, no legislation is now likely in the foreseeable future. Instead, a voluntary Code of Practice *Age Diversity in Employment* has been produced urging employers to utilise the huge resource pool of older workers who over the next ten years will represent more than a quarter of the workforce. Despite this, however, ageism is still very much in evidence in job advertisements.

The problem lies with stereotyped 'images' which imply certain abilities, or lack of them, associated with age, such as:

- **In your twenties:** you are likely to be more career-minded, fitter, have fewer family or financial commitments, more prepared to put your work before play if necessary, highly mobile and can live life at a fast and furious pace.

- **In your thirties:** you are likely to be well into your career, have good all-round work experience, have a family and a mortgage, looking for steady financial returns, have a partner who is also working to help maintain the family's standard of living, have a less flexible approach to mobility and other demands on your time and energy besides work.

- **In your forties or older:** you are likely to be established in your career, seeing your children through the last few years of their education, reluctant to move, resistent to new ideas, less prepared to put work before leisure and less vital or energetic.

There is probably a grain of truth in such stereotyping, but like all generalisations, this does not apply to everyone. There are always exceptions.

Unfortunately, you can be discriminated against on the grounds of age even when there is no mention of an age requirement in the advertisement. Stereotyping in such circumstances has become an automatic response. An employer looking for someone with flair and vitality is unlikely to consider anyone over 30. You can be too young for a job as well, particularly if it is aimed at someone with maturity and experience.

Be aware of this 'hidden agenda' as you read advertisements. See if you can spot when a stereotype is being sought.

If you apply for a job outside your age range, or where an age range is not specified but *is implied*, you have to think up ways of getting round these problems by emphasising you have got what it takes. This is assuming of course you are in a position to do this, and not pretending you can take on a work load which will ultimately defeat you.

Where you live

It has already been mentioned that if you are looking for a job outside your immediate geographical area, you must check adverts to see what financial help is on offer if you need to move house to take up the job.

Some adverts are quite clear about who should apply. For example, 'Only local applicants will be considered' is about as blunt as you can get, but there are other more subtle approaches. For instance, 'You are likely to be already living within daily travelling distance. . .'. This boils down to the same thing and there is little hope of any relocation package being offered. If you decided to apply, you would need to make it clear you understood you would be meeting relocation expenses from your own pocket.

Relocation packages in adverts are a good indicator that living outside the immediate area will not be an obstacle to your application.

Replying to box numbers

These leave applicants completely in the dark about the company or business offering the job.

There are occasions when this is perfectly acceptable, especially where a company is planning to expand into a new geographical or product area without forewarning its competitors. A reputable company in this position usually goes to some lengths to give potential applicants a good description of the type of business involved.

But what are you supposed to make of the following advert? It raises more questions than it answers.

CAR MECHANIC WANTED

Must be prepared to work flexible hours
Good rates of pay for the right person

Apply:
Box 30, Broscom Gazette
Broscom

Why is a box number being quoted in this instance instead of the proper name and address of the firm? What is meant by 'flexible hours'? What are the 'good rates of pay' referred to? As no experience or qualifications are mentioned, just who is the 'right person' for the job?

Suspicions are inevitably aroused. Is this a small-time business with no idea about the essential legal requirements of employing staff? Is it a *bona fide* business at all, or one which at best could be described as slightly shady, or at worst downright criminal? Could you be involved in cosmetic work on 'write-offs' before they are off-loaded at car auctions, or acting as nurse-maid for stolen vehicles?

Look at adverts with box numbers carefully, and ask yourself whether there appears to be a valid reason for not quoting the company's name.

Basic salary and remuneration packages

The term 'attractive remuneration package' is still popular, despite the taxation of many of these so-called 'employee benefits'.

There are all manner of perks available these days which make comparisons between one employer and the next almost impossible to calculate in monetary terms, such as:

- private health care for the whole family
- profit-sharing
- company car
- non-contributory pension and life assurance schemes
- telephone expenses
- preferential mortgages
- preferential car loans.

There is, however, a downside to these perks. The tax levied on company cars, health care schemes and preferential mortgages, for instance, is quite considerable. What appears on the surface to be an attractive package is not quite what it first seems. Basic salary remains the best guideline. It is safer to regard anything else as icing on the cake and be wary of placing too much value on fringe benefits.

Negotiable salary or no salary quoted

Situations where there is no salary mentioned or where it is described as negotiable, or 'commensurate with experience', put you at a disadvantage.

In the first instance, you do not necessarily know whether your potential employer has a generous pay policy or not. How can you enter into negotiations without knowing the upper and lower limits in the employer's mind?

There is also the lingering suspicion that a company which is not prepared to put its cards on the table over something as basic as salary is out to get someone on the cheap.

In the second instance, where salary is offered 'commensurate with experience', you are equally as blind: you have no idea what measure is being used to gauge your experience, or what the base level of remuneration is to begin with.

Commission only

You need to give very careful consideration to what you are letting yourself in for if you apply for a job which offers commission only. The enticing figure of '20K in your first six months' can mask the fact that you might have to work all hours of the day and night to get even remotely near this figure. You also have to be sure you are not expected to finance the setting up of your own office – or anything else.

Any advert which promises easy money for comparatively little effort or outlay should be treated with the greatest possible caution.

On target earnings

This formula is often found in adverts for sales reps. Popularly reduced to the letters OTE with a grand salary figure attached, this is another danger zone. The figure quoted is the salary you will receive *provided you meet the targets set for you*. Like the job where you receive commission only, your targets might be almost impossible to achieve so your financial return could turn out considerably less than you bargained for.

Some employers do quote a minimum salary and go on to say that your OTE could reach £X. This at least gives you a sound basis on which to weigh up the pros and cons of pursuing an application, even if you find out later that the targets are unrealistic and well beyond your reach.

Salary bands

A job which offers a range of salaries, usually linked to the phrase 'salary commensurate with qualifications and experience', always looks attractive because you immediately start quantifying your qualifications and experience and pitching the salary near the top end of what is on offer. This phrase, however, is practically meaningless and leaves employers in a good position to offer you the lowest they can get away with. In a job market overflowing with good candidates, your experience and qualifications may in fact count for very little. The employer may have already set the upper level at which the job will be offered, and it will be nowhere near the upper limit of the salary supposedly available.

In these situations, use the lower figure quoted as the basis for any offer which might be made. If this is below the figure you identified as your basic minimum, you either have to discount applying for the job, or take a chance on upping the amount once you've got it in your grasp. This does not always work, however, because you are gambling on no other candidate coming a close second who is prepared to take the lower figure.

HOW TO RESPOND

Once you spot a job vacancy you feel confident you can fill, don't blow your chances right from the start by making the wrong approach in reply to the advert. **DO WHAT YOU ARE ASKED TO DO**. It is quite staggering how many applicants don't.

READ the advert thoroughly.

● If it asks you to apply by letter, **DON'T** send a CV or ask for an application form.

- If you are sent an application form, DON'T send it back blank with your CV attached.

- If you are asked to apply in your own handwriting, DON'T submit a typewritten or word-processed version.

- If it tells you no telephone enquiries will be accepted, DON'T phone.

- If you are asked to submit your CV on disk using specific software, DON'T use an incompatible format.

- If the basic requirements of the job are in the advert, DON'T write asking for further details – you won't get them.

It cannot be emphasised strongly enough that you *must* make contact with your potential employer in the way you are asked to – *and no other*. There is nothing guaranteed to irritate a recruiter faster than someone who can't or won't be bothered to follow a simple instruction. You may very well be the best qualified person for the job in terms of your skills and experience, but you will never be given the chance to show that you are.

WHO DO THEY WANT?

Set out on pages 62 and 63 are a selection of advertisements which are typical of the type of jobs advertised in local papers. The higher paid posts in Fig. 11 (7) and (8) would also appear in the appropriate trade/professional journals and possibly a national daily as well. They vary in style, content and information provided. Some give obvious clues about the type of person they are trying to attract; others are less precise.

Read each advert thoroughly. Write down the points in the advertisements which you believe are important:

- relating to the organisation offering the job, the job content and wage/salary offered; and

- an outline of the ideal candidate in terms of skills, qualifications, experience (and age).

The following notes are a rough guide to help you.

Trainee Draughtsperson – Fig. 11 (1)
This advert is quite specific about who should apply and what skills they should have if possible, but there is little other definite information. It gives

Young Person required for the position of

**TRAINEE DRAUGHTSPERSON/
GENERAL OFFICE DUTIES**

for large commercial catering equipment company. Basic drawing skills would be an advantage. Please apply in writing to

**BRUNSKILLS
CATERING EQUIPMENT**

Mellingground, Off Penrullock Road,
Kirkby Oswald, Northmorland TU10 6TH

 SALESPERSON

Required to work with our team, selling new and used vehicles.

Experience in selling would be preferred, but all applicants will be considered. The ideal applicant should be smart, self-motivated and hard working.

Salary dependent on experience and includes bonus and profit sharing schemes.

Apply in writing, giving full particulars to: Mr S. C. Elliott, Managing Director, Graham and Elliott Ltd., Uppergate Road, Ellenby, Northmorland TU8 7HV.

 KIRSTIE'S GARAGE LTD
39 Castlegate Road, Thorsby

Due to retirement, we require a skilled

Motor Mechanic

to join our team
Good rate of pay and working conditions
The applicant would also be required
to attend breakdowns in the evening.
Excellent rate of pay.

Please apply to:
Bob Wilson
After Sales Manger
Tel: (019293) 367888

➍ MANAGER/ESS

Required to run our busy Fast Food Restaurant in a new venture in the Ellendale area opening this summer. We need a competent person with suitable experience who is not afraid of hard work and is able to improve turnover and standards. We offer a good salary with bonus. Apply in writing with CV and references to:

**Box 630
Ellenby Herald, Ellenby**

➎ Northmorland Constabulary

SENIOR SECRETARY

Salary: Scale 3

This post is based at the Police Headquarters, Ingleton Hall, Ellenby. Applicants should have relevant typing and shorthand qualifications, together with secretarial experience ideally at a senior level.

Job descriptions and application forms available from: The Personnel Officer, Ingleton Hall, Police Headquarters, Ellenby TU8 8JV.

Striving to be an Equal Opportunity Employer

Fig. 11. How to read job advertisements. You may find it useful to keep a bookmark in these pages for ease of reference later.

WANTED
PART-TIME TELEMARKETING EXECUTIVE

A training company based in Stoneyhampton offers:

A good basic salary with performance-related bonuses.
Negotiable working hours. The chance to make the role permanent.
Please phone Nigel Temple on 015307 76767 any Friday in July
between 10.30 a.m. and 7.30 p.m. if you meet **ALL** these criteria:

- Money-motivated and determined to succeed
- Proven success and experienced in telemarketing
- A good administrator
- Mature and able to work with little supervision
- GCSE (Grades A–C) in English Language

ELLENDALE COLLEGE
requires a
CATERING MANAGER
to manage the expanding catering operation
Salary Scale 4/5

The successful candidate will have responsibility for:

- Financial Control
- Training and Assessing
- Statutory Requirements.

Applicants should have previous experience of the catering
industry and hold appropriate qualifications.

For further details and application form, E-mail: d.moss@ellendale.ac.uk or Tel:
01944 6793 (24 hr)

⑧ **Ellendale District Council**
CHIEF EXECUTIVE'S DEPARTMENT
S O L I C I T O R
Salary Grade PO41-44

Ellendale District comprises one of the most beautiful parts of the country with its main cen-
tres of population the market towns of Ellenby (the administrative centre), Kirkby Oswald,
Penrullock and Thorsby.

Accountable to the District Solicitor, you will be responsible for the day to day management
of the Legal Section comprising the Council's licensing, land charges, conveyancing and
Committee administration functions. You will attend main committees of the Council, provide general legal advice and represent the council as an advocate. You must be able to communicate effectively at all levels. Previous local government experience is preferred and the
successful candidate will have demonstrated sound professionalism and a good track record.
The Council operate a generous relocation scheme.

Application form and further details from the Corporate Services Officer, Town Hall,
Ellenby, Northmorland TU8 3SD Tel: (01944) 3434 (Ext. 269). (24 hour)

The Council is an equal opportunities employer and operates a non-smoking policy.

Fig. 11. How to read job advertisements – continued.

the overall impression of being rather impersonal and there is no named person to contact or write to.

The job is described as being a *Trainee* Draughtsperson. Training must therefore form part of the job. General office duties are expected as well. What could these be? They could possibly include filing, tidying the stationery cupboard, answering telephones, making tea, stoking the boiler, or running errands for more senior members of staff.

The company is described as *large*, so they should be well-known locally and their line of business is stated, so you should be able to find out more about them by looking up the various reference books in your local library (mentioned in Chapter 2).

The way to apply for the job is clearly set out.

There are no rates of pay mentioned, but the type of job indicates these are likely to be on the low side.

The ideal candidate

● Late teens, possibly early twenties.

● Will have basic drawing skills, although this is not absolutely necessary.

● Will be able to show a willingness to undergo training to improve or acquire skills.

● Will demonstrate some understanding of what is involved in office work and what aptitudes this would need, such as neat writing, a methodical approach, ability to answer the telephone, ability to mix well with others and so on.

● Will show willingness to take on any other duties as and when necessary.

● Will show some sign of having researched into the company and its products – and be interested in them.

● Will have put all this into a well-constructed and well-presented letter.

Salesperson – Fig. 11 (2)

Graham and Elliott Ltd are more interested in headlining the job on offer than themselves. The style of the advert is straightforward and slightly formal – Mr S. C. Elliott, rather than Steve Elliott, for instance.

Their business is set out in the first paragraph.

They have a sales team.

They are looking for some experience, but are not inflexible about this. They make particular mention that *all* candidates will be considered.

They state precisely what they are looking for in the ideal candidate as well as experience.

There is no clue as to what level of pay is on offer, but the existence of profit sharing schemes as well as bonus payments gives the hint of an enlightened employer.

There are clear instructions on how to apply.

The ideal candidate
If you were Mr Elliott, who would you see as an ideal candidate? Would they be male or female? Is this another form of stereotyping? Could anyone else do the job? How could they demonstrate they were self-motivated and hard working?

Motor Mechanic – Fig. 11 (3)
Kirstie's have put their name at the top, so they must place some value on being well-known and possibly well-respected as an employer. They go to some lengths to explain why the post is available. The previous post-holder has just retired, implying many years' service as a matter of choice. The style is chatty and informal, and there is a named person to contact.

There is no indication as to age of the most likely candidate, but the use of 'skilled' implies a reasonable length of experience – possibly five years.

The job will be one of an existing team.

The pay and conditions are described as good (and in the case of pay this is repeated) but not specified.

Flexibility in working hours is expected.

Although Kirstie's address heads the advert, the directions on how to apply seem to indicate this should be done by telephone rather than in writing.

The ideal candidate
- Likely to be at least in their twenties.

- Will demonstrate a wide range of experience with a variety of vehicles.

- Will be able to work with others.

- Will be able to demonstrate a willingness to be called out at weekends or in the evenings.

- Will know something about Kirstie's business and reputation.

- Will be able to put all this over on the telephone in a friendly informal manner.

Manager/ess – Fig. 11 (4)

What do you make of this advert? What impression do you get of the company behind it? What other questions come to mind?

The ideal candidate

How do you think it would be possible for candidates to illustrate their competence, experience, their acceptance of hard work and their ability to improve turnover and standards?

Senior Secretary – Fig. 11 (5)

This is a fairly standard advertisement of its type. What details are missing? How might you expect to find out more about what skills are required? Is there any particular category of person being encouraged to apply?

The ideal candidate

Without the job description it is impossible to be precise about the level of qualifications being asked for, but what sort of picture do you get of the ideal candidate as a person? Is this a stereotyped image? Who else could do the job just as well?

Telemarketing Executive – Fig. 11 (6)

Stoneyhampton is not in Northmorland. What image do you think this company is trying to give? What is your impression of the job on offer?

The ideal candidate

Who do you think would be ideal for this job? What age do you think they would be? What clues are there that give you that impression? How could applicants show they met all the criteria asked for?

Catering Manager – Fig. 11 (7)

What word in this advert makes you think this job will grow in responsibility? How would you go about finding out more about this job?

The ideal candidate

Without the job description, the skills and aptitudes the perfect candidates should demonstrate can't be defined precisely, but what sort of background would you expect candidates to have? What would the key tasks of their last job have been, and at what level?

Solicitor – Fig. 11 (8)

This is a typical local government advertisement. What clues are there that this post is being widely advertised? Who are they trying to appeal to? Could you apply if you were a smoker?

The ideal candidate

Who do you think will be interviewed for this job? What expertise will they be able to offer and how will this have been gained? What age do you think most candidates will be? What reasons will they give for wanting to work in Ellendale? (The beautiful area is one which is taken for granted. Pick others relating to the job on offer.)

PRACTICE MAKES PERFECT

The more you read adverts, the quicker you will be able to analyse their contents. Remember the emphasis is on **READING** and not **SCANNING**. Remember too that you are identifying not only what you are looking for, but just as importantly, what employers are looking for. You can't afford to waste your time, effort and money applying for jobs where you do not possess the skills, experience or qualifications expected.

ACTION CHECKLIST

- Identify which are the best sources of job vacancies to meet your job search.

- Keep up-to-date with alternative or current trends in job titles.

- Read advertistments carefully – DON'T SCAN.

- Be alert to the flexible or inflexible requirements for the ideal candidate.

- Understand the generalisations behind stereotyping and how these may affect your applications.

- Recognise the possible pitfalls in financial packages on offer.

- Follow instructions on how to make your applications correctly.

- Be aware of possible pitfalls in using the Internet for recruitment purposes.

4

Composing a Letter

Where your first contact with a prospective employer is to be by letter, either:

- requesting an application form, or

- attached to your CV, or

- as an application in itself

There are a few simple, basic rules to follow.

Remember, recruiters are busy people. In small firms, recruitment is often down to the manager or owner; in larger organisations, recruitment is only part of the workload of a personnel department. Often there are literally hundreds of applicants for one job.

Imagine a pile of more than 200 letters. If each one received one minute of the recruiter's time it would take around three-and-a-half hours just to complete the first sifting. This represents almost half a day's work. No recruiter can afford to spend that amount of time on the initial stages of the weeding-out process. So forget about being given a minute – your letter is likely to be dealt with in *seconds*.

BASIC RULES

If your letter is only going to be the centre of attention for a few brief moments there are some very obvious rules you should follow.

Dos
- DO make sure what is on the paper is legible.

- DO make sure the finished product looks attractive.

- DO use a larger size of paper rather than several smaller pages if you have a lot to say.

Don'ts

● DON'T write on any old piece of paper that comes to hand.

● DON'T use lined paper torn out of a notebook.

● DON'T use paper which is deeply coloured or has pretty patterns or borders.

Some employers no longer reply to letters which in their opinion are ill-conceived or poorly presented: they are simply not prepared to waste time and money on them. You want to be confident your letter will produce a positive reaction and you are half way to achieving this if your letter has the following:

● a symmetrical layout which is visually attractive; and

● all the relevant information contained on one sheet, or two at the most.

Be prepared to spend time on your letter. There are eight stages:

```
PLAN – DRAFT – EDIT – REDRAFT –
CONSIDER – RE-EDIT – REDRAFT – COMPLETE
```

With practice you may be able to cut out stages six and seven – but always make sure you are absolutely satisfied with what you have produced.

MATERIALS TO USE

Using the right pen
If you have been asked to apply in your own handwriting – or if there is no guidance one way or the other, and you don't have access to a typewriter or word-processor – use a fountain pen, preferably with black ink. Ball-point pens and their many variants rarely produce a good finished product and are usually less easy to read.

Black ink is better and clearer to read than blue, and has the added advantage of photocopying well. It should go without saying that unless you are applying for a job in the creative field, green or purple ink is generally regarded as unacceptable.

Typewriters and word-processors
If the jobs you are applying for involve typing skills, always type your letters, making certain your ribbon is not past its sell-by date.

Don't use a typewriter if you are inexperienced. A badly typed piece of work with a poor layout, evidence of corrections and barely legible print is as bad as a scruffy piece of handwriting.

Word-processors – provided they are used properly – can produce the best finished product, but don't spoil an excellent layout with a faded printer ribbon, or draft-quality print-out. If you have a variety of different fonts on your printer, choose the plain, easy to read styles rather than the more 'artistic' variations.

Always use single spacing for content and double spacing to separate paragraphs.

What writing paper?

You can use a standard writing pad for brief request letters to be written by hand (avoiding lines and dark colours) and it is sometimes acceptable to use pale coloured paper too in these circumstances. But if you want to play safe, stick to white.

If you are using a typewriter or word-processor *always* use A4, plain white, good quality paper.

PUTTING TOGETHER A SIMPLE LETTER

This section deals with the initial enquiry letter and the covering letter you send with a completed form or CV.

The basic layout

There is no single correct way of laying out a letter. Often it comes down to what looks right on the size of paper being used, and the medium chosen, *ie* whether it is handwritten or typed. Whichever style you choose, however, there are some basic rules you should follow. Always include:

- your address and postcode (fax, telephone number and E-mail address if applicable)

- the date

- any reference which you have been asked to quote

- the name and address of the recipient including postcode.

The choice of layouts can be either:

1. Your address, telephone number and date in the top right-hand corner; any reference and the recipient's name and address slightly lower on the left (see David Chadwick's letter on page 82) or

2. The date (with any reference immediately below it) in the top left-hand corner; your address, date and telephone number at the top right; with the recipient's name and address at the *end* of the letter in the bottom left-hand corner. (See Sarah Walker's and Gordon Donnelly's letters on pages 84, 85 and 86.)

There is a lot to be said for adopting the second method. By keeping the reference and date out of the way, they don't add to the length of 'dead' space taken up by your address. Similarly, by placing the recipient's name and address at the end, the main content of the letter – which is the important part as far as you are concerned – occupies centre stage, rather than being pushed towards the bottom of the page where it loses its impact.

This isn't simply the 'looks good' factor: the human eye tends to focus one third of the way down a page quite naturally, therefore the main body of your letter should occupy this vital space rather than the recipient's address.

Dear . . .
How should you begin?

The best advice is – 'Do what the advert tells you': For example, if you are asked to write to Mrs Williamson, begin the letter 'Dear Mrs Williamson'. If you are asked to contact the Personnel Officer, start with 'Dear Sir or Madam' (*not* Madam*e* – a common error which implies the lady is either French, or that perhaps she runs a house of ill-repute!).

If you are instructed to write to 'The Personnel Officer' and you want to show you have taken the trouble to find out who this person is, you can contact the company – *unless the advert expressly tells you not to* – and ask for the name of the person in question. If you are applying to a large organisation, however, responsibility for recruitment is often delegated to someone further down the line. In this case your efforts may go unnoticed.

Heading or no heading?
Putting the job title as a heading has the advantage of making life easier for whoever opens and sorts the morning mail. In a small business, it immediately highlights the fact that you are a job applicant, not a customer or client; in a larger organisation where more than one job is being advertised, it immediately identifies which post you are applying for.

Contents of your letter
Ideally, your simple letter should be no longer than two or three paragraphs. Remember this is not the application itself, so keep it brief. It should contain the following:

- an introduction and reason for writing

- any specific information (if relevant)

- a conclusion.

Your first paragraph
When the letter is asking for an application form, or it is attached to a CV, simply state that you are applying for the job and where you saw it advertised. (Employers are keen to know which form of advertising produces the best results.)

If you are returning an application form, thank whoever sent it and acknowledge any additional information which came with it.

Your second paragraph
If you are requesting an application form and further details, do so here and sign off.

If this is a covering letter, draw attention to the attached papers so that should they become separated, a search can be mounted for them.

Also use this paragraph to highlight any specific points you want to emphasise in your application. This is *not* the place, however, to add any further information *which should have been included as part of the form or CV.*

Your third paragraph
This is simply to round off the covering letter. Say you are looking forward to hearing from whoever you are writing to, but don't imply you expect to be interviewed, or say anything which suggests you are calling the tune. Nothing is further from the truth, and pushiness – as distinct from confidence – is rarely appreciated.

Employers used to acknowledge receipt of applications, but this practice has now almost died out. If you want to be certain your application has been received safely, enclose a stamped self-addressed postcard with the job title and name of the firm on the reverse, and ask for this to be returned to you. The end of the letter is the best place to make this request.

Signing off
This should match the formal or personal approach you adopted at the start of your letter.

| Dear Sir/Dear Madam . . . | Yours faithfully |
| Dear Mrs Williamson . . . | Yours sincerely |

These are the only two acceptable methods you should use to sign off. Anything else is unsuitable.

Make sure you print your name under your signature for the sake of clarity, and add Mr, Mrs, Ms or Miss if you have a name which is uncommon or likely to cause confusion.

EXAMPLES TO STUDY I

The following examples are based on the advertisements appearing on pages 62 and 63 in Chapter 3.

Martin Thomas (41)

Martin worked for 23 years at Pearson and Trueman Limited, a medium-sized engineering company based in the Midlands with over 1,200 employees. Martin joined them as a Catering Assistant, gaining promotion until he finally became Catering Manager. Six weeks ago the factory closed down. Martin has relatives living in Northmorland and at their suggestion he has decided to apply for jobs in the area. He has a BTEC National Diploma in Catering, and from his personnel and financial experience with Pearson and Trueman he feels confident he could tackle either of the catering jobs on offer – Fig. 11 (4) and (7).

Martin last applied for a job when he started at Pearson and Trueman and he is badly out of practice. On the following pages are examples of letters he has written in response to both advertisements. Read through the comments made on each. Add anything else you may feel is relevant.

In his response to the position of Manager/ess (Fig. 11 advert 4) Martin's presentation in Fig. 12 is inadequate: there are too many errors and omissions which may jeopardise consideration of his CV.

(1) No phone number.

(2) The date should have been written in full.

(3) The letter should have begun 'Dear Sir or Madam'.

(4) Where is the new restaurant? He does not say. There may be several new outlets opening in the UK. He does not live in Ellendale, so his preference might not be identified.

(5) There is no mention of where he saw the advertisement.

228 Broxborough Rd
Wood Bank
Halesbury
BX12 4 DT ①
11 - 6 - XX ②

Dear Sir ③
I would like to apply for
the post of Manager in
your new Restaurant. ④⑤
Attached is my CV and
the names and addresses
of two referees. ⑥
Hoping to hear from you
shortly. ⑦
        Yours Sincerely ⑧
        Martin Thomas
                ⑨
⑩

Fig. 12. Poor example of an application letter sent in response to advert 4 (Fig. 11).

(6) He should have reinforced his experience and qualifications here.

(7) This ending presumes too much.

(8) He should have used 'Yours faithfully' (with no capital letter for 'faithfully').

(9) His signature is difficult to read and he is relying on his recipient hunting this out from his CV.

(10) He has omitted the recipient's address. This is still important, even if it is a box number.

Figure 13 is a better effort. Martin has chosen a larger piece of paper to prevent the finished product looking cramped and untidy and the general appearance of the letter is one of symmetry. He has also remembered to include some of the points he missed in his earlier effort. He has not mentioned where he saw the advertisement, but in this case it is not necessary, as he is writing to the *Ellenby Herald* anyway. However, he has still made

11 June 20XX   228 Broxborough
                               Wood Bank
                                 Halesbury
                               ① BX12 4DT

Dear Sir or Madame ②
    I would like to apply for the
post of Manager at your new
restaurant opening in Ellendale
this summer.
              ③
    I have eight years experience
as a Catering Manager and hold
a BTEC National Diploma in
Catering. Attached is my CV
together with the names and
addresses of two referees.
    Looking forward to hearing
from you in due course.
              Yours faithfully
              Martin Thomas
                (MARTIN THOMAS)

Box 630
Ellenby Herald
Ellenby
Northumberland
TU8 3JV

Fig. 13. Better example of an application letter.

75

14 June 20XX

228 Broxborough Road
Wood Bank
Halesbury
BX12 4TD

Tel: 018370 72644

Dear Mr Turner

CATERING MANAGER

Thank you for your letter of 12 June 20XX enclosing an
application form and further details in connection with the
above post at Ellendale College.

Enclosed is my completed form together with a stamped,
self-addressed postcard which I would be grateful if you
could return to me to confirm the safe receipt of my
application.

Looking forward to hearing from you in due course.

Yours sincerely

Martin Thomas

Mr C A Turner
Principal
Ellendale College
Millthorpe Road
Ellenby
Northmorland
TU8 7TY

Fig. 14. Example of typed letter. This refers to Fig. 11 (7).

some mistakes and needs to be less rushed in his style of writing which tends towards being a scrawl.

In the last example, in response to the advertisement for a Catering Manager (Fig. 11 advert 4) Martin phoned the Principal's Secretary asking for an application form and further details. When these arrived, he discovered the Catering Manager not only had the responsibility for overseeing the efficient operation of meals provided to 600 students, staff and visitors, but also the smooth running of the stock control and purchasing of the Faculty of Catering. As this Faculty is considered one of the best in the UK, the job of Catering Manager is obviously one of considerable importance.

Under these circumstances, Martin decided to arrange for his covering letter to be typewritten. He also adopted a printed style of handwriting on the form itself to ensure an eye-catching neat presentation.

(1) He has forgotten his phone number again.

(2) He has misspelt 'Madam'.

(3) His punctuation is shaky.

WRITING LETTERS OF APPLICATION

Although this method of application is often thought to be the easiest, it is by far the most difficult to do well. Why is this? There are three main areas of difficulty.

1. Not knowing what to put in.

2. Putting in too much.

3. Putting in details which are irrelevant.

Applicants repeatedly let themselves down by not giving sufficient thought to what the letter should contain. Remember your aim is to sell your skills to your prospective employer, not to boost your own ego. A remarkable number of applicants go into great detail about their achievements but make no attempt to explain how these could be usefully employed in the workplace.

PREPARING A ROUGH DRAFT

A rough-out in the first stage is absolutely vital. Aim for a finished product with three or four paragraphs of *relevant* information. Every word must count. There must be no room for waffle.

Ideally, your letter should be on one sheet of paper and no longer than two – with the writing on one side only. This can be a problem if you are writing by hand – this always takes up more space than the printed word.

Layout and style

Re-read the advice given earlier in this chapter on basic layouts (page 70) and check who you are supposed to be writing to and address them in the proper manner. Decide whether or not you want to use the job title as a heading before you begin the main part of your letter.

Your first paragraph
Keep this to express your interest in the job on offer and where you saw it advertised.

Your second and third paragraphs
This is the meat of your application. Begin by studying the advert, the job description and any background information on the company which you may have been sent or which you have gathered from the library. Begin to get the feel of the job itself and the company offering it.

Highlight the key words or phrases in the advertisement as you did in the exercise at the end of Chapter 3, and any additional points which have come to light if you have received a more detailed job description. This way you will be quite clear about what the employer is looking for.

Note the style of the advertisement. Is it formal and stiff, or informal and chatty? Mentally adjust the way you are going to phrase your application to match. You are more likely to succeed if you mirror the style adopted by the recruiter. Don't go too far with this, however, or you may find yourself slipping into bureaucratic stiffness, or flippancy.

Go through your Personal Data File and pick out your *best examples* to highlight experience, skills, and qualifications to match what is wanted. Don't forget to bring in any *relevant* portable skills you have acquired outside the work place.

Illustrate the personal qualities the employer wants to see in a candidate by using examples from both your work and leisure experiences as described in Chapter 1. Stick to what is being looked for – not what you want to boast about.

AVOID meaningless phrases and clichéd jargon. You simply have no room for anything which does not inform or enlighten.

Final paragraph
This wraps it all up. By all means offer to expand on any aspect you have mentioned either at interview or over the phone. NEVER offer 'additional information' on the same basis, however, as this implies you have omitted some relevant facts which should have been included in your letter. And lastly, express the view that you are looking forward to hearing from them – but don't say when.

Signing off
Follow the guidelines set out earlier in this chapter and remember to print your name underneath your signature and mention your status if you have a name which could belong to either gender or is in any way unusual.

Editing your first draft
If your rough draft is too rough, put it into better shape before beginning the editing process.

Once it is in an acceptable form read through it critically. Remember you have to say everything in the briefest way possible.

Check the content. You are looking for RELEVANCE and the POSITIVE APPROACH.

1. Do the skills and qualifications you mention relate to the job in question? If they don't, cross them out.

2. Have you used long-winded sentences? If you have, find a more concise way of expressing yourself.

3. Have you apologised for any shortcomings, or drawn attention to them? Don't. If you lack any qualities being sought don't emphasise them, put forward positive alternatives instead.

4. Have you included any down-beat words, such as *unfortunately, failed, redundant*? Remove these.

5. Have you included trendy phrases which could be expressed in simpler English? Remove them – you can't afford the space.

6. Have you used vague generalisations qualified by such words as *usually, occasionally, sometimes*? Be precise. Quantify.

7. Have you repeated yourself? Don't.

Now write it all out again. This time, check the following:

- spelling
- grammar
- punctuation.

So much for content. Now you know what you are saying, are you producing the right effect? Read the letter aloud. What is the result? Does it sound positive and vital, or is it halting, lame, unsure of itself? Have you used too many 'dull' verbs? (Remember all those exciting words you used to identify key tasks in Chapter 1 – *assessing, monitoring, checking, informing etc*). Do too many of your sentences start with 'I'? Re-draft your sentences to produce a varied and interesting structure.

Finally, check the size of your finished draft. Is it going to fit comfortably onto the paper? If you are going to send a typed copy, how does this look when it's finished? Can you improve the layout?

THE COMPLETED LETTER

When you are completely satisfied with the draft, read through it once more. Often, you spot an obvious error you failed to notice previously.

When you have finished:

- sign your name at the bottom (with the printed version underneath)

- keep a copy for reference

- fold the original no more than twice

- use a good quality envelope to put it in

- correctly address the envelope, not forgetting the postcode

- send it well in advance of the closing date

- remember to keep your copy letter, advert, job description *etc* in your Job Record File and mark up your Progress Sheet.

EXAMPLES TO STUDY II

In this section, three applicants are applying in response to Graham and Elliott's advertisement, Fig. 11 (2), page 62. Their backgrounds are very different and they all have something to offer, but none of them is the ideal candidate. What qualities did you identify in the ideal candidate on page 64?

To be successful at selling, you need several attributes: your personality has to be right; you have to be able to communicate; you have to be knowledgeable and enthusiastic about your product; and you have to be persuasive.

David Chadwick (19)

David is single and living with his parents. He left school at 16 with mixed GCSE results. His one ambition has always been to work with cars. For the last three years he has been working as a trainee mechanic at 'Fit for the Road', a reputable local small-scale repair garage. He has passed his driving test and obtained the City and Guilds 3830 Motor Vehicle Mechanics qualification. All his savings have gone into purchasing a 1970s Magna Merlin which has become something of a collectors' car. He spends much of his spare time overhauling this and has recently joined the local Merlin Owners Club.

In the foreseeable future 'Fit for the Road' cannot offer David any promotion prospects and he wants to move on. He could try for the experienced mechanic's job at Kirstie's Garage – Fig. 11 (3), page 62 – but although he still enjoys the mechanical side of the job, he would prefer to move over into sales. Graham and Elliott operate the local franchise for Magna cars and David is keen to take this opportunity.

David is not very experienced in writing letters but has taken the trouble to find out the right way to go about them. He is very conscious of his lack of selling experience and realises he must not draw attention to this. Instead, he wants to emphasise his enthusiasm for the Magna range, his proven mechanical knowledge and his willingness to learn to be a salesman.

David's letter is set out overleaf. Has he achieved what he set out to do? Would you have done it any differently?

Sarah Walker (32)

Sarah is divorced and has two children aged 11 and 9. She worked as a petrol pump attendant and sales assistant in her father's garage before her marriage, and her ex-husband Bob was one of the salesmen employed there. After he developed a drink problem, their marriage gradually fell apart and Sarah has been on her own now for six months. During this time she has managed to organise good child-care arrangements for her children after school and during holidays.

Sarah stayed at home while both the children were under school age but then began selling cosmetics on a part-time basis as an Avalon agent. She has done extremely well in this job and is now recognised as the best agent in the region. Although Sarah enjoys her job, she does not want to sell beauty products full-time and would like to try her hand at car sales. She has a good background knowledge of the trade from both her father and ex-

46 Ellenbank Court
Low Town
Ellenby
TU8 3BC
Tel: 01944-5659
16th April 20XX

Mr S. C. Elliott,
Graham and Elliott Ltd,
Uppergate Road,
Ellenby TU8 7HV.

Dear Mr Elliott,

I would like to apply for the job of salesperson you advertised in the Ellenby Herald.

I am 19 years old, of smart appearance, enjoy hard work and like talking about cars. I have a clean driving licence.

For the last three years I have worked for Fit for the Road in Hope Street as a trainee mechanic, carrying out general repair work and regular servicing on cars and vans of all makes. I have passed my City and Guilds 3830 in Motor Vehicle Mechanics and would very much like the chance to move into sales where my technical knowledge would be useful.

My main interest has always been in Magna cars. Last year I bought a 1976 Magna Merlin and now belong to the Ellendale Merlin Owners Club. I like to keep up to date with the latest range of Magna models and collect specification data and test drive write-ups from 'My Car' and 'Motoring Mania' magazines.

I am very keen to join your salesteam and hope you feel able to offer me an interview.

Yours sincerely
David Chadwick
(DAVID CHADWICK)

Fig. 15. David Chadwick's application letter.

husband and has attended basic car maintenance courses at evening classes. She has also enrolled for an Advanced Driving Course.

Sarah owns a second-hand car bought from Graham and Elliott and was impressed with the way the sale was handled.

Sarah knows she will have no problem convincing an employer she would be an asset to the sales team: she is well turned out as all Avalon agents are and can illustrate her sales ability by listing her successes. Her main obstacle, she believes, is to persuade Graham and Elliott she is capable of switching from beauty products to car sales. To do this she feels she will have to emphasise her background knowledge of the motor trade and bring out her self-motivation. Her other concern is that Graham and Elliott do not at the moment have any female sales staff, despite the trend to attract women into this type of job. Because of this she does not want to draw attention to either her divorce or her children in the letter, and would prefer to discuss these, if necessary, at an interview, where she would be far more able to handle these topics successfully.

Sarah's letter is on the next two pages. Has she managed to overcome the problems she identified? Could she improve her letter?

Gordon Donnelly (46)

Gordon is married with a son in his second year at university. Gordon began his career as a car salesman, working his way up to becoming a manager of a small firm before finally breaking away on his own. For the last 16 years he has run his own garage in Penrullock with a staff of four, selling petrol and good quality second-hand cars, many of them Magnas. The business had a steady turnover but began to decline with the opening of the Penrullock bypass two years ago which dramatically reduced petrol sales. Gordon was eventually forced to close the business four months ago. He needs work badly to see his son through his last year at university, and is looking for employment in an area where he feels confident he can succeed.

Gordon's background is ideal, but he knows he faces three possible problems:

1. The failure of his business, which is a negative factor.

2. His age, although maturity is often a plus point in selling cars.

3. The difficulty in persuading an employer he can adjust to being part of a team of employees instead of the boss.

He knows he will have to play down the negative side of his application and concentrate on his self-motivation and the conviction that he is adaptable

16 April 200X

23 Drovers Way
High Side
Ellenby
TU8 6RJ
Tel. No. 01944_3729

Dear Mr Elliott

SALESPERSON

I would like to be considered for the above
vacancy advertised in the Ellenby Herald
this week.

I am 32 years of age with good sales experience
and background knowledge of the motor trade.

For the past five years I have worked part-time
as an Avalon agent selling beauty products
in the Ellenby area, and for the second year
running have won the regional Best Sales
Award. I have also already exceeded my
sales targets for the first six months of
this year.

Up until my marriage in 199X, I worked as a
sales assistant for my father at Thorsby
Hall Garage. My husband was also employed
as a car salesman and I learned many of
the selling techniques I now use from his
experience. At the same time I have been
able to keep myself informed about
developments in the trade from brochures
and other trade literature.

Fig. 16. Sarah Walker's application letter.

During the past two years, I have successfully completed basic and advanced courses in car maintenance at Ellendale College to add practical experience to my selling skills. I have also enrolled with the Northmorland Police to take the Advanced Driving Course in June.

I own a Magna Madeira which I bought from your showroom last August, and I would welcome the opportunity of joining your professional full-time sales team.

Yours sincerely
Sarah Walker (Mrs)

Mr S.C. Elliott,
Graham and Elliott Ltd.,
Uppergate Road.
Ellenby,
TU8 7HV.

Fig. 16. Sarah Walker's application letter – continued.

16th April, 200X

The Millhouse
Trenton Lane
Pennullock
TU12 3GB
Tel: 01944-86773

Dear Mr Elliott,

I am writing in response to your advertisement in the Ellenby Herald for the vacancy of a salesperson.

I began my career in car sales with Harris Motors 28 years ago and was Salesman of the Year three years in succession before being made Assistant Manager in 198X and then Manager in 198X. I started my own business in 198X selling petrol and good quality second-hand cars at the Cross Roads Garage, Pennullock, a business I built up and carried on until earlier this year.

The reputation of Graham and Elliott is well known to me through my long association with the local motor trade, and I would like to offer my services as a member of your sales team. I am prepared to work on a trial basis for no remuneration to demonstrate my ability to meet your requirements, if you feel this would be useful.

I am available for interview at any time and look forward to hearing from you.

Yours sincerely

Gordon Donnelly
(GORDON DONNELLY)

Mr SC Elliott
Graham and Elliott Ltd
Uppergate Road
Ellenby   TU8 7HV

Fig. 17. Gordon Donnelly's application letter.

86

enough to revert to a subordinate role.

Looking through Gordon's letter on page 86, do you think he has managed to do this? Would you have added or omitted anything else?

If you were Mr Elliott, would you invite all three to be interviewed? Who is your favourite candidate on paper – and why?

WRITING A SPECULATIVE LETTER

Some companies welcome speculative letters; they even go to the trouble of categorising good quality applicants and keeping them on a data base, using this as the first port of call when a vacancy arises.

Letters written to prospective employers 'on spec' and not in response to a job advertisement have to be tackled differently. In this situation, you have nothing specific to aim for. Instead, it is up to you to identify possible openings – and to convince the employer you would be able to make a useful contribution to the firm. To do this successfully, you need to know a great deal about the company, its products or services, operational structure, staff numbers and so on. Ignorance in this case is not bliss – it's just plain ignorance.

All too often speculative approaches, particularly from graduates, are unfocused and have the emphasis the wrong way round. The employer is not there to help you achieve personal self-development. He or she will be paying you for your contribution towards developing the business. If during the course of this process, the experience and training you gain help your own development, all well and good – but this is a by-product as far as your employer is concerned, not the prime motive for your employment.

Put yourself in the chair of the Managing Director of an expanding firm of good quality book shops. Read through the speculative letter set out overleaf. The reference to the enclosed CV is irrelevant: the letter says it all.

1. How many basic errors are there in presentation?

2. What impression does this give?

3. What reasons does Joanne give for wanting to join the company?

4. What benefits does she think she could bring to the company?

5. What evidence is there that she has researched the products and structure of the company?

6. How does she relate her experience and qualifications to what the

36 Kelsington Avenue
Esterby
Sherbridge
SH4 8YU

Tele: 973854

Dear sirs

I am writing to enquire as to whether there are any
situations vacant within your company. I have recently
graduated from Broxborough University where I gained a
degree in Sociology and am now interested in following a
career in book retailing. My primary aim is to join a
company in which I can gain experience whilst using the
skills I have gained so far.

My extra-curriculum activities whilst at university
included sailing, going to the theatre, cooking and swim-
ming. I am a bright, mature and highly motivated young
woman who enjoys new challenges. Since graduating I
have also completed a word processing course which has
brought me up to date with office technology.

I enclose a copy of my CV for your perusal.

Thanking you for your time, I await a reply at your
earliest convenience.

Yours faithfully

Ms Joanne D James

Encs.

Fig. 18. Poor example of letter enquiring about job vacancies.

company might be looking for?

7. How does her list of hobbies relate to book retailing?

8. What evidence does she supply to back up her description of herself?

9. Would you spend time sifting through her CV to see if there was any reason why you should employ her?

In a nutshell, Joanne has wasted her time. She has made little effort to persuade her prospective employer she has anything to offer. It is very unlikely that she will even get a reply.

ACTION CHECKLIST

● Aim for the 'looks good' factor in letter writing.

● Choose the right format and paper for the type of letter you are writing.

● Adopt a writing style which reflects the tone of the advertisement.

● Plan, draft, edit and redraft until your letter looks and sounds right.

● Choose the best layout to keep your letter to one or two pages of A4 at the most.

● Know the accepted form of address for opening and closing letters.

● Recognise the differences between application letters in response to advertisements, letters accompanying application forms or CVs, and speculative letters.

● Develop and practise attractive, readable handwriting.

5

Completing an Application Form

WHO USES FORMS?

Application forms probably represent the least loved aspect of any job search. They are still widely used, however, particularly for public service appointments and where vetting procedures for new employees are carried out. Local government, the Civil Service, National Health Service, college appointments and the police service are just some examples.

Application forms do not follow any particular pattern and variations are as numerous as the organisations using them. Consequently it is necessary to talk in general terms about how to tackle them.

The one thing they all have in common, however, is they want answers. You cannot pick and choose what information you want to include: your age; maiden name; marital status; number and age of children; your employment history down to the last dot and comma, even details of your parents and spouse in some cases are requested. Some applicants feel the amount of detail wanted is more than is required – and would certainly not be included as a matter of course in a CV. This topic will be discussed later in the chapter.

There are both advantages and disadvantages to application forms.

Advantages of application forms

1. **You do not have to spend hours planning your layout**. This is already done for you.

2. **Your data is already available**. If your Personal Data File is complete you can simply transfer basic details onto the form. Tedious perhaps, but a relatively simple process.

3. **Recruiters can compare applicants more easily**. They know everything will be in exactly the same place on every form. The initial sifting process is therefore made much easier.

Disadvantages of application forms.

1. **Some forms specifically instruct you to complete all sections**. This means you have little chance to present yourself as you would wish. You are highly visible – warts and all.

2. **The space provided is either too much or too little**. This is a persistent problem. It can lead you into the double trap of either reducing information to match the space provided thereby omitting important factual details, or expanding the data to fill an over-large section with irrelevant padding.

3. **Your 'sales pitch' is restricted to such sections as 'Additional information'**. This is the main gripe against forms. Your ability to put yourself across in a positive and vital manner is limited, especially if you have to include less desirable information elsewhere without room for adequate explanation.

WHY ARE FORMS USED?

Application forms have taken on new roles over the years. Originally they were simple recruitment tools. Now they are often the basis for setting up employment records, training programmes, payroll and pension details *etc* – which perhaps helps to explain some of the seemingly impertinent questions asked in them.

They have also become management tools as companies and organisations strive to become equal opportunity employers, monitoring who responds to their advertisements and in what numbers. Questions on ethnic background, disability and gender are increasingly appearing as part of the form on an anonymous tear-off slip or separate sheet.

Forms have one other highly significant role. At the end there is usually a declaration to be signed which says that to the best of your knowledge, the information provided is both true and complete. This is a crucial statement. Falsification of information can not only disqualify your application, *it can be grounds for subsequent dismissal*. You must never put yourself in this situation.

This is particularly important if you have any criminal convictions or cautions and you are asked to declare them. You must be absolutely certain the type of job you are applying for does not demand you declare *all* these, regardless of whether they are 'spent' or not. In sensitive employment areas, criminal records are always checked and the **Police Act 1997** when it comes into force will contain provisions which give employers wide ranging powers to do this.

Some forms contain a medical questionnaire, particularly where a job can only be done by someone who is physically or mentally fit. But health generally is increasingly becoming a recruiting factor. Anyone with a history of above-average absence through ill-health , rather than disability, will find it increasingly difficult to secure a job in the future. Staff absence to an employer equals additional costs in either lost production or extra payments to provide job cover.

YOUR AIMS WHEN COMPLETING THE FORM

Your aims should be:

- neatness
- conciseness
- completeness
- interest.

The way to achieve all four, despite the limitations of forms in general, is to do the following:

1. Read the form thoroughly. Understand what you are being asked to do under each heading.

2. Make a photocopy, not only to use in the drafting stage, but also to keep as a copy of your finished article.

3. Remind yourself of your aims throughout the process.

4. Write down *all* the answers to every section on scrap paper first to allow for any amendments before completing the final draft.

5. When you complete the original, remember to follow the instructions given, *ie* use black ink, block capitals, *etc*.

NEATNESS PAYS

Handwritten or typewritten?

Just as a badly presented letter gets the three-second-brush-off, so does a badly presented application form.

Neatness must be your prime objective. Your form must have that 'look good' factor. Unfortunately, where you could achieve this by using a typewriter or word-processor when writing a letter, application forms are less obliging. Most are printed and the boxes allocated for answers rarely coincide with the spacing of an average typewriter. This can result in disaster: split words; over-runs; or different alignment in different boxes. The effect is the same – an unattractive piece of work. Stick to handwriting – it's safer.

What do you do if your natural handwriting is poor? Be prepared to develop a printed format – specifically for application forms. The easiest to use is the basic style adopted by primary schools: it is clear and easy to read, and usually complements the printing on the form itself. This simple hand does not take long to learn and is worth the effort when the result is attractive and pleasing to read.

Choice of writing implements

If you can, use a fountain pen, or a good quality ball-point which does not 'blob'. Felt-tips or cheap alternatives rarely produce a good result. Some also contain ink which spreads illegibly into the fabric of the page as though you were writing on blotting paper.

Always use black ink, even if this is not specifically asked for. Application forms are usually photocopied for one reason or another, and black ink makes a crisper copy than blue. Other colours of course are totally unacceptable.

BEING CONCISE

Dealing with limited space

This is one of the main problems you are likely to encounter.

Try to avoid having to attach additional sheets to your form, even if this is encouraged. Additional pages are always in danger of becoming separated or lost.

If space is very limited, however, use the diary entry format as follows:

- remove any definite and indefinite articles – 'the's and 'a's;

- use participles – that part of the verb ending in '-ing' – to reduce the number of 'I's in your sentences; and

- cut down on long-winded phrases. Use 'while' instead of 'during the course of', or 'because' instead of 'as a result of', and so on.

Making the content count

Be precise in what you say.

Get rid of hazy words such as 'very', 'largely', 'generally', 'occasionally' or 'mostly'. Quantify. Put down specific times, numbers, events or whatever. Make every word count towards giving a clearer picture.

Use only *relevant* data. Relevance keeps cropping up, but it remains the biggest stumbling block to most applications. Stop yourself from squeezing in what *you* want to say. Keep asking yourself if this is what *your prospective employer* wants to see.

Choose positive and vital sounding words. Put plenty of action into whatever you are describing.

BEING COMPLETE

Some people feel very strongly the structure of application forms means highlighting some aspect of themselves which might prejudice their application. Is it possible to soften this apparently rigid structure? The answer is 'yes – sometimes', provided you do not distort the truth until it becomes a lie.

If you do decide to omit any information, you must recognise this could jeopardise your application, or provide a talking point if you are invited to interview. This latter point may be what you intended, but it may also deflect the main thrust of the interview away from more important topics and distort the outcome.

CONTENTIOUS SECTIONS

Your previous name

Sometimes appearing as 'Maiden name' on forms in the past, this was expected to be completed by every married woman. Many organisations no longer include this on their forms with the realisation your previous name is totally irrelevant to your ability to do the job. If you need to be vetted, however, your previous name is required so that police and other records can be checked.

Nationality and place of birth

These headings can still cause considerable resentment.

Many firms now use them as part of a recruitment monitoring process, and go to some lengths to explain their reasons. This is the only justifiable reason apart from situations where you are applying for a position which requires positive vetting. If there is no explanation for the appearance of these headings on a form, it usually means they are a hangover from a less enlightened age. Under these circumstances, the chances are that no one would notice if you left them blank.

Age

If you have already been asked for your date of birth, arguably your age should not be needed: it smacks either of age discrimination, laziness on the part of the recruiter, or a lack of numerical ability. If you are trying for a job where your age could inhibit your success, you are more likely to fail by leaving the space blank – and irritating the recruiter – than by putting it in and adding a qualifying term. A 'vigorous 50 year old' or a 'mature and caring 24 year old', may still not get through the first sifting, but there is always the chance you might raise your recruiter's interest enough to give you a second glance. Careful humour – but please note the word *careful* – can sometimes be an asset.

Your marital status

You can argue there are only two marital states – single or married. All the rest can be fitted into one or other category irrespective of whether you are separated, widowed or divorced. If you feel this interpretation is helpful in your personal circumstances, then by all means use it. Remember, however, that if you get offered the job, you might need to be more precise with the payroll department, particularly if direct payments to an estranged spouse have to be made from your pay packet.

Theoretically, marriage should have no bearing on your ability to do the job. Perhaps with this in mind, and with the gradual shift away from formal marriage into unofficial partnerships, this heading now appears less frequently than in the past.

Number of children and ages

Having children is a perfectly normal human activity – except where some employers are concerned. As with marriage, how many children you have and what age they are should have no bearing on how you cope with your job. In practice, however, it is quite another matter.

Discrimination, particularly against women, in this respect is still very much in evidence. If you are a mother with young children it is almost universally assumed that if they fall ill, you will need to take time off to look after them.

If you are a father, your children can pose a different problem: it is assumed their educational needs will restrict your mobility.

Neither of these assumptions might be correct in your own case. State why not if you feel having to declare the existence of your children might jeopardise your application.

YOUR EMPLOYMENT DETAILS

Basic factual headings such as:

● name and address of employer

- position held/job title
- duties and responsibilities
- reasons for leaving
- salary

were covered in Chapter 1 when you compiled your Personal Data File (page 18).

Breaks in your employment

These are a particularly thorny problem. Most forms ask you to give the dates when you worked for a particular employer. Dealing with time spent in prison has already been discussed on page 28 in Chapter 1, but there are other gaps which you might need to explain.

If these are short-term, such as a holiday taken between the end of one job and the start of the next, or a delay in finding employment which lasted a couple of weeks, then you are justified in not mentioning these.

Longer-term gaps which cover several months or more are best explained. The trick is to do it in the best possible manner, particularly if you have suffered unemployment, redundancy or taken early retirement.

- Use positive terms.
- Keep it brief.

The following are a selection of possible reasons:

- job-hunting
- seeking redeployment
- seeking re-employment
- voluntary community work
- overseas voluntary work
- family commitments
- study break.

All these statements have an up-beat, active feel to them. This is what is needed. By using them, you also come across as a more attractive personality: someone who doesn't have a chip on their shoulder even if life has given you a rough ride. It can't be stressed enough – the more you emphasise your misfortunes, the greater they become.

Too many jobs

This topic was also covered in Chapter 1 (page 18). Some application forms allow considerable space for previous employment. If they do, don't be tempted to list all your jobs just because you have the space to do so. Keep similar posts lumped together in the distant past. Don't draw attention to how many you have had.

The right chronological order

Always check how you are being asked to record your employment details. Is it the last job first and the first job last – or vice versa? If you are given a free hand, **start with the last job first**. This is your most recent work experience and therefore the most relevant. Give this the greater proportion of available space and don't draw attention to less important jobs by making a meal out of them.

If your last job was in any way out of the ordinary run of your career pattern, perhaps as a stop-gap, reduce details to a minimum and concentrate on the last full-time permanent post which is relevant.

ADDING INTEREST

Headings such as 'Additional information', 'Reasons why you are applying for this post', 'Why do you feel this position is for you?' or 'Hobbies and interests' give you the opportunity to turn a dull application form into something entirely different – the bait with which to hook your prospective employer.

Application forms are great levellers, reducing candidates to the same format. Given the choice, recruiters would prefer to find one candidate who stands out from all the rest: this makes their job much easier. The outstanding candidate not only gets the chance of an interview, but also goes into that interview with positive expectations lodged firmly in the recruiters' minds. The 'Halo Effect' is already at work.

What you should include

These are the only sections on the form where you are not expected to put down absolutely everything. Sadly, this is precisely what happens in many cases. Before you know where you are you have either bored your recruiter rigid, or worse, raised questions about your suitability where none existed before.

If your interest in Anglo-Saxon archaeology doesn't demonstrate your ability to do the job, it has no place on your form, no matter how engrossing you find the subject; neither has your skill with a floor buffer if you are applying to be a bookkeeper; nor your stamp-collecting if you are applying to be part of a vivacious sales team. Everything you include should relate *first and foremost* to the job.

On the other hand, **never** leave these sections blank: it implies you have nothing to say for yourself.

Read through the original advertisement again. What are the skills being sought? What type of person are they looking for? How can you demonstrate you have these qualities which make you the right person for the job? Here you have the opportunity to put forward other examples of your skills and abilities you have not had the chance to bring to light elsewhere on the form.

Go back to your Personal Data File, hunt out from your pastimes any relevant examples to support and give added interest to your application.

If you don't have all the experience, skills or qualifications being asked for, this is the place to emphasise your portable skills gained outside the workplace: your motivation to learn or adapt *illustrated by examples* (saying so is not enough), and your enthusiasm for the job.

Make as many rough drafts as you need to get it right. It should flow; it should sound enthusiastic; it should use the descriptive words in the advertisement wherever possible; it should whet the recruiter's appetite to know more.

Hobbies and leisure activities

Use this section carefully. Theoretically, recruiters are supposed to be looking for candidates with a good mix of interests outside the workplace.

This may be true in some cases, but don't put in anything just to manufacture this balance. If your hobbies all tend towards the physical, don't add 'Reading' as a counterbalance just because you think you should – particularly if your reading is restricted to the sports pages of the newspaper. Recruiters are an odd bunch: they are just as likely to quiz you on this as anything else if you land an interview, and you could find yourself out of your depth. The same goes for sports if you are not a 'sporty' person. Don't be tempted to redress the balance by including sports you last played in your third year at secondary school.

If you have an imbalance, don't keep adding to it by listing every single sport or hobby you do. Two examples should be enough and these should only be used to illustrate some aspect of your suitability for the job: leadership skills; team work; individual merit; self-development; self-motivation – whatever the advertisement is asking you to demonstrate.

Be careful too about including the more physically demanding pastimes. No employer wants an employee who spends the majority of the working week recovering from hang gliding accidents at weekends. You may be very proud of your prowess, but your enthusiasm for hard physical activities could work against you in the employment field – unless you are applying for a job which demands outdoor training skills.

GIVING REFERENCES

Most application forms expect you to provide the names and addresses of at least two referees sometimes three. Organisations have differing attitudes to who constitutes a 'referee'; some want one of your references to be your last employer (or a recent employer) as well as a personal referee who knows you from a different perspective; others don't specify categories, but are more interested in how long the person has known you. You should already have a small pool of people prepared to act as your referees listed in your Personal Data File, and subsequently kept them informed of your progress. Those who you would like to act for you should now be told you are applying for this post.

Most employers provide referees with details of the job vacancy so they can comment on the applicant's suitability. When you contact your referees, mention any particular aspect of your application which you believe they could emphasise from their knowledge of you either as a person, or as an employee.

THE FINISHED FORM

Once you have completed your rough work, *check spelling and grammar*, and rewrite any parts which need improvement.

- Transfer all your rough work onto the photocopied form in pencil to check spacing.

- Revise and adapt this if necessary.

- Complete the original form in the manner requested.

- Read through and check for unintentional errors.

- Write a covering letter (as suggested in Chapter 4).

- Attach a self-addressed stamped postcard for acknowledgement that your application has been received.

- Use a good quality A4 or A5 envelope.

- Address this properly.

- Never fold the form more than once.

- Post it in good time before the closing date for applications.

- Keep your copy form attached to the advert and any other papers in your Job Record File and mark up your Progress Sheet.

EXAMPLES TO STUDY III

The following two case studies relate to the advertisement for the post of Senior Secretary with Northmorland Constabulary in Chapter 3, Fig. 11 (5), page 62.

The key tasks listed on the job description are:

1. Providing secretarial duties for the Assistant Chief Constable.

2. Dealing with all confidential matters from heads of departments, other forces and agencies.

3. Attending meetings and court hearings, taking shorthand notes and typing minutes and evidence.

4. Scheduling all appointments, meetings and interviews for the Assistant Chief Constable and making necessary arrangements.

5. Liaising with:
   - senior management, members of the force and other forces face-to-face
   - members of the Policy Authority and Senior Officers of the County Council by phone
   - members of the public by phone.

Skills requirements include:

- 50 wpm typing
- 120 wpm shorthand desirable with a working knowledge of word-processing
- secretarial experience, preferably at a senior level.

Daniel Andrews

Daniel is married with one child. He left school at 18 with two A-Levels, and decided to go into the retail trade. He was taken on as a Trainee Manager by a supermarket chain and worked his way up to Assistant Manager at 25.

NORTHMORLAND CONSTABULARY

APPLICATION FOR EMPLOYMENT – CIVILIAN DIVISION

Post applied for ...... SENIOR SECRETARY ......

PERSONAL DETAILS (Block letters please)

Surname (Mr/~~Mrs/Miss/Ms~~) ANDREWS .... Forenames DANIEL JAMES

Home address... 22 HILL TOP ROAD, ... Date of birth: 17 MAY 1966

..... HIGH SIDE, ELLENBY, ... Tel: Daytime 09448-8332 1

NORTHMORLAND ..Post code. TUB 3RJ ... Evening 0944 - 6312.

QUALIFICATIONS including school exams, degrees, diplomas, professional
exams etc with dates obtained)

1998-99 : RSA Word processing - Stages 1+2 (Credit)

1995-96 : RSA Typing Speed Test - 50 wpm
       Shorthand Stage 2 - 100 wpm

1986 : Inst. of Grocery Distribution Certificate

1984 : 2 'A' Levels (English, Economics)   1982: 6 'O' Levels

EMPLOYMENT HISTORY including any gaps with explanations

From	To	Employer's name & business	Position and duties of job
1996	Pres.	BOUNDLESS HORIZONS CHARITABLE TRUST Adventure holidays for the disabled	ADMINISTRATOR : Providing secretarial duties for Warden; dealing with daily correspondence; arranging weekly team meetings and taking minutes; liaising with other charities + Social Services Depts; confirming bookings; + holding confidential medical records of visitors.
1994 1984	96 94	– Retraining following STOCKWELL STORES LTD Retail Food Chain	spinal injury – TRAINEE + DEPT. MANAGER : 1984-91 · ASSISTANT MANAGER: 1991 - 94 ; overseeing and organising stock control + deliveries, staff rotas + security with other Asst. Manager; answering customer queries and complaints ; running staff suggestion scheme.

Fig. 19. Daniel Andrews' application form (continued overleaf).

ADDITIONAL INFORMATION giving details of other experience or skills relevant to this job

In 1998 I was elected parent governor for Ellenby Junior School. My duties include confidential work associated with staff discipline and recruitment, and liaising with senior officials of the County Council Education and Treasurer's Departments.

During my time at Stockwells, I attended in-house training courses designed to teach staff the interpersonal skills necessary to handle customer complaints and queries, both face-to-face and over the telephone; the importance of good communication and effective time management.

OTHER INTERESTS including hobbies, leisure pursuits etc

Desk-top publishing: After being approached by the Town Council in January 1998 I now produce the Council's Newsletter on a regular monthly basis.

Basketball: Since 1996 I have been a member of the Northmorland Hospital Spinal Injuries Unit basketball team (The Spinners) taking over as Captain in 1998.

REASONS FOR APPLYING FOR THIS POST

My experience both inside and outside the workplace has provided me with expertise in up-to-date office practice, secretarial and administrative skills. I now feel able to offer the maturity and discretion necessary to carry out the duties attached to this senior post in an efficient and responsible manner.

DECLARATION

I declare that the information I have given is to the best of my knowledge true and complete.

Signature ...D.J. Andrews............... Date...20 June 20xx

mf

Fig. 19. Daniel Andrews' application form – continued.

Three years later, a car in which he was a passenger was involved in an accident. Daniel suffered spinal injuries which left him confined to a wheelchair.

Unable to return to his former career Daniel was encouraged by his wife to build on his previous office experience. During two years of convalescence, he taught himself the basics of shorthand and typing, went on to attend evening classes and passed the first stage examinations. Armed with this success, he obtained a job as an administrator with a Trust set up to organise adventure holidays for the disabled in and around Penrullock.

Since then Daniel has continued his training in office skills and mastered word-processing and other IT skills. Although he enjoys his job, it concentrates on disability and he would prefer to move away into a more able-bodied environment, something he has consciously done with his social life where possible. He believes his office experience could easily transfer into the role of a Senior Secretary, particularly as the job description shows there is a large slice of personal assistant work involved which he does already.

Daniel realises he has three hurdles to cross:

1. Being a man, he is not the immediate stereotyped image of a secretary.

2. He is disabled and although the advert indicates Northmorland Constabulary is an equal opportunities employer, theory and practice are often worlds apart.

3. His experience of confidential work practices is low-key compared with what might be required.

Look through Daniel's draft application form overleaf. How well do you think he has done? Would you do anything differently in his case?

Comment on Daniel's application

Daniel has concentrated on aspects of his jobs and additional information which demonstrate his relevant abilities and portable skills. He has also used terms from the job description where he can and 'action' words.

He has placed his qualifications in reverse order to accentuate the skills he has recently acquired and has managed to play down his disability without obscuring it, at the same time adding an element of interest – his role as captain of the Spinal Injuries Unit basketball team.

He has also given a very up-beat set of reasons for wanting to apply for the job emphasising what he can offer rather than what he wants.

Overall, Daniel gives the impression of being a positive individual rather than someone beaten down by circumstances.

Marion Hartley

Marion is married with a grown up family. She returned to work 15 years ago on a part-time basis. During this time she obtained her shorthand and typing qualifications. Once her younger child was at secondary school, she returned to full-time employment. She obtained a shorthand-typist's job in the Treasurer's Department of Ellendale District Council where she later became temporary secretary during the absence of the postholder on maternity leave. This helped her to secure the job of secretary to the Corporate Services Officer, a post she has held for the last six years. Marion enjoys her job and has a good social life outside the workplace which includes membership of a highly successful competitive country dancing team, as well as acting in a secretarial capacity for a local charity.

The Council is now considering restructuring its departments. Corporate Services is likely to be absorbed and put under the direct control of the Chief Executive, and Marion fears her job is in jeopardy. She is therefore looking elsewhere with a sense of urgency. The job with Northmorland Constabulary seems an ideal opportunity for her.

Marion has not applied for a job on the open market for ten years. She knows this will make things difficult for her, but she is confident her range of experience and skills which match the requirements of the job description very well will make her the ideal candidate.

How do you feel Marion has coped with completing her draft? Would you do it differently?

Comment on Marion's application

Marion has produced an application which relies too heavily on qualifications and general experience. Her list of duties is obvious, and she has done nothing to give herself the edge over other candidates with similar qualifications. She gives no additional information on skills outside the workplace, such as her secretarial role for Help the Infirm, repeating instead some of the information she has already given elsewhere.

Her biggest mistake is mentioning possible departmental reorganisation as a reason for applying for the post. This gives the impression she is looking for any alternative rather than aiming for this job in particular.

Her list of other interests does nothing to advance her cause: it is mundane for the most part and unstimulating. She has missed the opportunity to show herself as part of a competitive and highly successful team which demonstrates good communication skills and commitment. Country dancing is vibrant and energetic, but none of this comes across in her application.

The lasting impression is of someone who is rather dull, stiff and over-anxious.

NORTHMORLAND CONSTABULARY

APPLICATION FOR EMPLOYMENT - CIVILIAN DIVISION

Post applied for ...SENIOR SECRETARY...................

PERSONAL DETAILS (Block letters please)

Surname (Mr/Mrs/Miss/Ms) HARTLEY.........   Forenames MARION..........

Home address...35 BIRCH AVENUE......   Date of birth 3-4-54...

NEW SPRINGS   ELLENBY..............   Tel: Daytime 01944-3434

...................Post code TUB 5DK.   Evening 01944-2601

QUALIFICATIONS including school exams, degrees, diplomas, professional exams etc with dates obtained)

1970 - 'O' Levels : English Language and Literature, French, History, Maths, RE and Geography.

1983 - R.S.A. Typing Stage 1; Shorthand Stage 1 (60 wpm)

1986 -   ..   ..   2 ;   ..   .. 2 (100 wpm)

1988 -   ..   .. Speed (60) ;   .. .. 3 (130 wpm)

EMPLOYMENT HISTORY including any gaps with explanations

From	To	Employer's name & business	Position and duties of job
1994	–	Ellendale District Council Corporate Services Dept	Secretary to Corporate Services Officer responsible for correspondence, memos, reports to Council and Committees; dealing with staffing matters; arranging meetings and interviews. I also have frequent contact with senior officers, councillors and the general public.
1991	1994	Ellendale District Council, Treasurer's Dept.	Shorthand/Typist: Rating Section Deputised for Secretary in 1986.
1987	1991	Renaissance Insurance	P/T Typist
1986	1987	Hall Dennes Estate Agents	P/T Receptionist
1974	1985	Family responsibilities	

mf

Fig. 20. Marion Hartley's application form (continued overleaf).

ADDITIONAL INFORMATION giving details of other experience or skills relevant to this job

In 1995 I took an 8-week course at Ellendale College on the "Principles and Basics of Word Processing".

My present position involves dealing with confidential correspondence and reports to the Council. It also includes extensive knowledge of word processing and a high level of shorthand capabilities.

OTHER INTERESTS including hobbies, leisure pursuits etc

I am an active member of the local branch of Help the Infirm.

I enjoy country dancing, reading, knitting, cooking, and gardening.

REASONS FOR APPLYING FOR THIS POST

As there is likely to be a departmental restructuring exercise in the near future, I am looking for a similar position where my experience and qualifications can be fully utilised.

DECLARATION

I declare that the information I have given is to the best of my knowledge true and complete.

Signature *Marion Hartley* .... Date. 21-6-XX .....

Fig. 20. Marion Hartley's application form – continued.

ACTION CHECKLIST

- Make photocopies of application forms for rough draft working.

- Aim for the 'looks good' factor.

- Use BLACK ink and a good pen for the finished product.

- Be both precise and concise to make the best use of available space.

- Complete all sections of the form which are essential.

- Adapt contentious sections *honestly* if you believe you must, BUT recognise this might jeopardise your application.

- Complete the employment history section fully starting with your most recent full-time job.

- Use positive terminology to cover any gaps or other areas of weakness.

- Only include *relevant* data in sections set aside for additional information.

6

Compiling a Curriculum Vitae

WHAT IS A CURRICULUM VITAE?

Curriculum vitae is Latin – it means the course of life – a biographical sketch, if you like.

In job vacancy advertisements it can appear in several disguises – its shortened form 'CV', 'full CV', 'Biodata', or transformed into 'Career history'. Strictly speaking, a 'Career history' is not a CV because it is limited to only part of your life – the world of work; it takes no account of your education, training, outside interests or portable skills.

The one thing a CV is not is an application form without the boxes. Anyone brought up on a diet of application forms will find compiling one hard work: it demands a different approach and very often a flexible layout of both headings and content.

WHAT YOU SHOULD AIM FOR WITH YOUR CV

To be most effective, a CV must:

● be clear and concise

● set out why you believe you are the right person for the job

● show what you can offer the employer.

There are too many CVs which don't achieve any of these goals.

Remember the word 'sketch'. The outlines should be there with the essential shading to give it depth, but not minute detail.

The advantages
The lack of rigid format allows you:

● flexibility in your presentation

- the opportunity to highlight the best of everything in your life and career

- the chance to leave out or tone down less favourable details which might prejudice your application.

The disadvantages
These are:

- not everyone is good at selling themselves on paper with no predetermined guidelines to follow

- the lack of set format can result in a poorly constructed CV which no matter how nicely produced will just not succeed.

POSSIBLE HEADINGS TO USE

Before you begin, look through the list of headings which follow. Think of these as a checklist rather than actual headings themselves. This applies particularly to all those marked with *.

Once you have stated your name, address and telephone number, the remaining headings can be used when and how you think best – *not necessarily in the order set out below*. There are some which, depending on your circumstances, you will not use at all.

Name *
Always put this in full, indicating which is your surname, either by using block letters or underlining, if there could be any doubt.

Address *
Use your main address. Any short-term alternative can be mentioned in your covering letter. This reduces the amount of space taken up on the page.

Telephone and E-mail address
State your daytime and evening telephone numbers if these are different.

Date of birth
This is best in full, *eg* 28 January 1961. You do not need to state your age.

Marital status *
You do not need to include this information. If you do, consider whether to reduce the data to 'Married' or 'Single'. (See page 95, Chapter 5.)

Children *

The same goes for this heading as for 'Marital status' – it is up to you whether you include this information or not.

Disability *

The Disability Discrimination Act has placed duties on employers not to discriminate against applicants on the grounds of their disability and to make reasonable adjustment to premises where a disabled person is the candidate best suited for the job. However, the law applies only to employers with 15 or more employees and some jobs are not covered, for example prison officers, firefighters, police forces and the Armed Forces.

Regardless of the size of the organisation advertising the vacancy, it is probably the wisest course of action to let a potential employer know if you consider yourself to have a disability. Many employers not covered by the Act are nonetheless prepared to follow the spirit of it. However, they would need to know if there were likely to be workplace difficulties arising from your disability or whether you would need a different interview venue, perhaps to allow better access facilities.

Profile *

This is not really a heading – more of an introductory statement. It should be brief, no more than two sentences, and is intended to provide an immediately pen-picture of who you are and what you have to offer, for instance:

- Mature lady with up-dated secretarial and language skills seeking re-employment after a career break.

- Enthusiastic and hard-working school-leaver with vacational catering experience, seeking first full-time permanent post.

- Young, energetic salesman with successful direct and telesales experience in interior design marketing.

Include in a profile any special skills or qualities mentioned in the advertisement to highlight your suitability for the post.

Professional qualifications

These should be kept separate from educational qualifications and should only refer to those which you still hold. If you are no longer licensed to practise a particular profession, do not imply you are.

Education and qualifications

If you are a mature applicant, leave out details of schools – these are irrelevant once you have a career history.

When listing qualifications:

● Put the highest level of qualification first (together with the year it was achieved).

● Reduce the rest to basic data or leave it out altogether if you hold a degree or its equivalent.

● DO NOT set out every single examination subject at lower levels. Group them together under a common heading and state the number of subjects passed. Less important qualifications should never swamp more advanced achievements

● DO NOT include any examinations you failed.

If you have just left school, don't be tempted to set out your examination successes in detail. This is not necessary. Your employer will only be interested in the numbers you passed, and whether these include English Language and Mathematics (GCSE Grades A-C). If the advert asks for a particular subject, then mention this. For example:

– GCSE: 8 subjects including Maths (B), English Language (B) and CDT Technology (A).

Training and short courses

Use this section to include any *relevant* additional training which would help your application. Again, note the word relevant. There is always the desire to show how much you know, what you have achieved, and the extent of your experience of this, that and the other, but if it is not relevant LEAVE IT OUT.

Career or work history

This should always be completed by placing your last position first. Re-read the advice given on page 96 of Chapter 5 on situations where your last job was in any way different from the rest of your career.

Key skills

This is a particularly useful heading if you have limited work experience. Here you can bring out your portable skills from pastimes, vacational or voluntary work.

If you have a career history, you can combine the skills from both the workplace and your pastimes.

Use the list of skills and abilities listed in the advertisement as starting points.

Interests
Only include these if they are in any way relevant to your application.

Reasons for applying
A brief statement under this heading means you do not have to include reasons in your covering letter, a plus point if the letter should get detached from your CV.

It also gives you the chance to show you have done some research into the employer's business and put your application into some sort of context. To do this, always substantiate your statements. For example, 'This experience would be beneficial to a building society *because* . . .' DO NOT imply you are only out to gain advantage for yourself. For example, 'My main aim is to join a company where I can gain additional experience . . .' No one likes to be made use of – and that includes prospective employers.

PRODUCING A GOOD CV

There is a bewildering mountain of advice published on how to produce a good CV – much of it contradictory. What is regarded as the perfect layout by one writer is rubbished by the next.

The only constant factors in all the advice offered are – a finished CV *must* be:

- typed, NOT handwritten
- as brief and informative as possible, preferably on one side of A4 paper, and certainly no longer than two
- immaculately set out.

How you achieve the ideal CV will depend on what you feel is right for you; that it says what you want it to say in the right place with the right effect.

The professionally produced CV
With increased numbers of people chasing jobs and more job applications dependent on CVs, there is a corresponding increase in the number of businesses producing CVs for people who do not want to tackle the task themselves.

There is no guarantee that such CVs will be any more successful than your own 'home-grown' variety – in fact, evidence would seem to indicate quite the opposite. They may meet all the criteria of a good CV, but they also tend to have an impersonal feel to them so that your personality is often missing from the finished article.

It is worth knowing that not many employers favour this type of CV, so if there is any suspicion yours has been produced for you, you run the risk of being seen as someone who can't be bothered to do the job themselves. This is not a very positive image.

DIY advice

As mentioned above, there is plenty available – including this book. Read as many alternative methods of producing CVs as you can. If you find a particular formula which appeals to you, then by all means follow it – but make sure you do not slavishly copy someone else's suggestions without questioning whether these are right for you.

The all-purpose CV

This CV is produced once, and copies sent out either in response to possible openings or 'on spec'.

The problem with this type of CV is that by its very nature it has to deal with generalisations: it is not focused to respond to any particular organisation or business. This does not matter where you are applying for broadly similar types of job with broadly similar types of employer. The reasons for your application can be included in the covering letter.

The danger lies, however, in using them in response to a particular job advert. Because the details are not tailored to meet the requirements of a specific job, they do not accentuate your most appropriate skills or abilities to give your application that extra lift. Consequently, they can sound very bland – or downright dull. On the Net, this type of CV only emphasises the lack of its refinement, particularly if you register your details on a site offering an E-mail job search. Your CV will be scanned by a program hunting for key words, either to pass it on to a potential employer or to provide you with a range of vacancies on offer.

Some applicants cram their CVs with a mass of details hoping to boost their chances of finding a job by this method. However, this approach is more likely to diminish your chances of success than improve them. Software programs are not selective in their approach. If you fill your CV with information which does not focus precisely on the type of job you are looking for there are two probable outcomes. Firstly, by being non-specific you will be deluged with unsuitable jobs which have been prompted by what the search program decided were key words. Secondly, your CV will be passed to potential employers who have absolutely no interest in you.

The individual CV for a specific job

This has to be the best format, even if it represents hard work for those without access to a word-processor. It is the essential approach for anyone wanting to change direction and set out on a new career.

The advantage of the individually produced CV is that it completely focuses on the job you are applying for, and can concentrate on targeting your skills more effectively. This applies whether you are applying for a job in the traditional way or by using the Net.

The vital focal point on a page

The human eyes naturally focus *one-third of the way down from the top of a page*. This is a vitally important piece of information. You MUST ensure that your most crucial piece of information *is at this point*. This is the place to put your Profile, your professional qualifications, the duties and responsibilities of your last job – whatever is most appropriate in your case to maximise your sales pitch. This is NOT the place to state you are married/ single, how many children you have, your primary education, or anything else which can only be regarded as unimportant to your application.

THE ROUGH DRAFT

You will probably need several shots at getting your CV just right. If you work your way through the draft stages carefully and thoughtfully, it may take a little time, but you are more likely to be satisfied with the finished result. Set yourself up with plenty of scrap paper.

Work your way through the following stages.

1. Read the advertisement and any job description.

2. List the qualifications, skills and qualities being sought.

3. Identify which of these are 'essential' or 'desirable'.

4. Check if there are any 'implied' requirements associated with the job, *eg* receptionist = good communication, pleasant personality, smart appearance, good telephone manner *etc.*

5. Extract from your Personal Data File the best examples of what is being sought from your 'Work experience or career history' section.

6. Repeat the process with your 'Pastimes' section to identify either additional skills to emphasise your suitability, or portable skills to fill any awkward gaps.

7. Look critically at what you have selected and remove anything which is not completely relevant.

8. Reread the advertisement and identify the *main* requirement of the job.

9. Aim to place your best examples of this at the vital focal point on page one.

LAYOUT

Main heading

There are differences of opinion over placing the words 'Curriculum Vitae' at the top of your first page. Some schools of thought say this is unnecessary and you should give your personal details top billing.

It's up to you. If you are short of space, you may well want to leave this out. If you feel your CV looks 'undressed' without its title, then put it in.

Personal details

Keep your personal details down to:

- name
- address
- phone number
- date of birth.

If you are applying for a job outside the stipulated age range, then demote your date of birth to a lower priority – preferably the bottom of page 1 (or page 2).

Adopt the same approach to 'Marital Status' and 'Children' – if you intend to include either of these headings – you will be very close to the all-important focal point at this stage.

Filling the focal point

This is where the CV wins hands down over the application form. YOU can choose what should fill this space. Usually it will be one of the following:

- personal profile

- professional qualifications or training
- educational qualifications
- employment record
- key skills (a combination of work and pastime data).

Which should you use?

Go back to where you identified the main requirements of the job. Which of the above headings contains the best example(s) of these from your point of view? Is there a description of the ideal candidate which would best be served by a personal profile? Are professional qualifications or training stipulated as being paramount? Is a certain educational standard absolutely essential? Is specific experience in a particular industry or business the crucial factor? Are skills being sought which you have already bunched together from both your work experience and leisure interests?

If you are producing a 'key skills' CV, you should not need to take up space laboriously setting out all your employment history in detail: this will only need to be a very brief summary.

What should follow

Lay out the remaining sections *you believe are relevant* to suit your data so there is some shape to the CV and not a random flitting from topic to topic.

'Reasons for applying' is a good way of rounding off so that your CV is not left hanging in the air.

At the end of the chapter are some examples of different CV layouts to study. The first is an unfocused CV which does not target the job in question. The others are variations of targeted CVs. These are not meant to be used as templates: their function is to set you thinking about what sort of CV you prefer and which layout would best suit your personal situation and the type of employment you are seeking.

OVERCOMING LAYOUT PROBLEMS

Space

This is always the main problem with any CV. There is usually far too little of it, particularly if you are a mature applicant with a busy and varied career behind you.

Unlike the application form where you are often obliged to list jobs meticulously, you do not have this restriction with a CV. Instead, if you are setting out your employment history, concentrate on the job or jobs you held during the last five years. If you have the space, you can afford to pick out the most salient points of the jobs you held five years prior to that. If not, lump the rest of your career history into an explanatory sentence. For example: 'During the 1980s I held a variety of service jobs in the hotel and catering industry.' This effectively tells the reader the level of the jobs involved and which area of business these were in. The same applies to any temporary or part-time employment which has only limited bearing on your present application.

If you adopt a narrative style, you can also effectively remove the need to explain away gaps in your employment which are not relevant to your application. Gaps which are relevant should be mentioned, but rather in passing, and not given star billing.

The 'look good' factor

If at all possible, try to place your sections or paragraphs so they are complete at the end of the page. This gives your CV a tidy, crisp presentational feel.

Much of the 'Look Good' factor will have to wait until you reach the stage of being able to produce a typewritten version of your work, but you may be able to see problems arising before you reach this stage. If you do, then sort them out sooner rather than later.

Finishing half way down the second page leaves the impression that something is missing. Rather than filling up your sections with irrelevant details, re-align your data so that each page has a similar amount. Then by careful use of spacing, you can produce a good looking product which still contains only data which is most relevant to your application.

DEVELOPING THE RIGHT STYLE

Most of the comments which follow have already been mentioned in earlier chapters, but it is important not to forget them here.

- Sound positive and vital.
- Sound interesting.
- Cut down on prose in cramped sections.
- Don't repeat data already given.
- Don't use the same verbs all the time – remember the list you identified in your Personal Data File.
- Cut down on the 'I's.
- Be specific, don't generalise.
- Highlight your achievements in areas the employer will want to see.

THE FINISHED PRODUCT

Redraft your handwritten work as often as it takes to be satisfied with the content. Once you feel comfortable with this, arrange for a typewritten draft to be completed and see if the layout is what you want. If not, rearrange this until you are satisfied with the result. Only when this process is complete are you ready to produce the final version.

The right format

Your CV should always be on good quality plain white A4 paper. If it runs to two sides, have this on a second sheet rather than print on the back of the first. Very often, printing on the reverse of paper can be seen from the front and spoils the presentation. If you are concerned about sheets becoming detached have the second page typed separately and a *good quality* back-to-back photocopy made. Poor quality photocopies or poorly aligned photocopies are not acceptable.

Don't overdo presentation: this can often work against you. Most recruiters do not want to wrestle with plastic or bulky folders. Keep it simple.

The covering letter

Always write a covering letter to identify which post you are applying for. This should be brief and along the lines suggested in Chapter 4, page 68.

Ready to go

- make copies of both your finished CV and covering letter

- use an A4 or A5 good quality envelope, properly addressed to the right person

- enclose your CV, *folding it no more than once*, together with your stamped, self-addressed postcard

- send everything off in good time before the closing date

- file copies of all your documentation together in your Job File

- mark up the necessary information on your Progress Sheet.

EXAMPLES TO STUDY IV

Mr Fisher owns an expanding wholesale office stationery business – The Paper Mountain – based in Kirkby Oswald. He has acquired an additional warehouse facility and wants to transfer his bookkeeping onto computer and employ a full-time bookkeeper/computer operator. He has placed the following advertisement in the *Ellenby Herald*.

**ARE YOU WILLING TO BE THROWN
INTO
THE DEEP END?**

BOOKKEEPER/COMPUTER OPERATOR
required for growing
wholesale stationery business

Computer experience essential
Knowledge of WISE programs an advantage

Send your CV to:
Mr J Fisher, The Paper Mountain,
Crookback Yard, Kirkby Oswald
Northmorland TU10 1GC

On the following pages are four of the CVs Mr Fisher received. Study these and the comments on them. What are your impressions of the applicants? Who would you interview?

Comments on Jennifer's CV
Jennifer's CV is neat – but that is all. She has treated it like an application form and it fails as a result.

1. **There are too many unnecessary headings**. This is distracting.

2. **The focal point concentrates on irrelevant details**. 'Nationality', 'Driving' and 'Schools Attended' do nothing to show she would be a successful bookkeeper/computer operator. These should have been omitted.

3. **The qualification data is too detailed**. All that was needed was: GCSE – 8 subjects including English Language and Maths.

   A-Level – 2 subjects (N grade is not considered a pass).

   Reference to her piano examination was irrelevant.

CURRICULUM VITAE

FULL NAME: Jennifer Elizabeth Wain

HOME ADDRESS: Chantilly, Elm Way, Penrullock, Northmorland TU12 5JU

TELEPHONE NO.: (019448) 86213

DATE OF BIRTH: 9th April 1976

MARITAL STATUS: Single

NATIONALITY: British

DRIVING: I have a full clean driving licence

SCHOOLS ATTENDED:
1987-1993 Penrullock Comprehensive, Horton Drive, Penrullock
1993-95 Ellendale College, Millthorpe Road, Ellenby

QUALIFICATIONS:

1993 GCSE

English Language	A
English Literature	B
Mathematics	C
French	C
History	A
Biology	A
Physics	C
Chemistry	C

1995 A Level

English	C
General Studies	N
Business Studies	E

ADDITIONAL QUALIFICATIONS:

Grade 6 Piano	Pass

EMPLOYMENT:

1995-96 Sales Representative TriplePlus Double Glazing Hamsbridge, E Midlands I was responsible for running existing customer accounts and cold calling to locate new business and generate further leads. I made my own appointments and organised my own time. I was also responsible for all administration relating to orders and customer correspondence. After working very hard to succeed I still found it difficult to sell double glazing and decided I did not wish to continue a selling career.

Fig. 21. Jennifer Wain's CV.

1996	**Packer** Ellendale Plastics Ellenby This was a temporary post
1997	**Secretary** Ellendale Plastics Ellenby I was responsible for general office organisation and answering the telephone. I also fed orders into the computer. This firm unfortunately went bankrupt two months later.
1997-98	**Cutter** Markham & Topham Ltd Wayleas Industrial Estate Kirkby Oswald I took this job to make ends meet and left to become a self-employed upholsterer.
1998 to present	Self-employed upholsterer. The business is not succeeding very well at the moment and I am looking for full-time employment again.
HOBBIES:	Playing the piano, painting, juggling and pony trekking. I also collect miniature china houses and decorated thimbles.

REFEREES:

Mrs T P Gresham
32 Birch Grove
Ellenby

Occupation   Director

Mr G J Wilson
19 Collingdale Lane
Hambridge
E Midlands

Occupation   Sales Manager

Rev G A Hallsworthy
The Vicarage
Penrullock
Northmorland

Occupation   Vicar

4. **The employment and reference data is poorly presented**.

● Space is wasted setting out addresses in this way.

● She does not list any of her working skills. Instead she gives a sketchy account of her responsibilities with too many 'I's.

● There is no attempt to show the scale of businesses she worked for or the number of customers she dealt with.

5. **There are too many negatives**. She draws attention to her 'N' grade; she found her first job hard; there are employment gaps and short-term casual employment; the firm 'unfortunately' went bankrupt (hopefully not because of the way she processed the orders); and finally she appears to have failed in her attempt to become self-employed.

6. **The list of hobbies is irrelevant**. How do these relate to the job?

Jennifer comes across as a directionless person clutching at straws. There is nothing here to show she would succeed at the job.

Comment on Karen's CV

Karen has been able to keep her CV down to one page. She has chosen to place her qualifications at the focal point because she feels these are the strongest part of her application. She has left out the subjects below C grade as she knows these are not usually taken into account.

Her previous employment experience is limited to some useful vacational work and two years as a trainee receptionist. The temporary nature of the trainee post is not stressed, nor is it obvious that she is currently unemployed. Instead she has concentrated on providing details on the size of the business, its range of services and the type of work she was doing and is now looking for. She has also demonstrated how well she coped by mentioning she worked on her own three days every week.

Karen's interests are typical of her age group. She knows from her friends that under 'Interests' they often include 'Enjoying an active social life'. She recognises this can produce a negative reaction on paper so she has stressed the positive aspects instead. Although these amount to the same thing, the effect is quite different. She has also purposely omitted mentioning her marital status: she currently lives with her boyfriend but they have no plans to marry at the moment.

CURRICULUM VITAE

Karen Louise **DUKES**   Date of birth: 24 May 1981

5 Mortimer Court
Kirkby Oswald
Northmorland TU10 6YP   Telephone: (01989) 92287

QUALIFICATIONS AND TRAINING

1998   Hotel Reception Course – passed in the following:
             RSA – Bookkeeping, English, Mathematics and
             Typewriting.

1997   RSA – Core Text Processing Skills – Pass

             GCSE A-C Grades
             4 Subjects including English

PREVIOUS EMPLOYMENT

1998-2000   **Junior Receptionist**, Ellenwater Hotel, Thorsby.
             This was one of two trainee posts to help young
             people develop additional skills to help them find
             employment, not necessarily in the hotel industry.
             The hotel has 20 bedrooms and a small conference
             centre attached. My duties included receiving guests
             and delegates, taking payments, preparing
             documentation for banking, learning to use the
             computerised accounting system, setting up
             conference audio/visual equipment with
             conference organisers and dealing with telephoned
             and written enquiries and bookings for both the hotel
             and conference facilities. In the second year I worked
             on my own three days every week.

1998   Vacational employment in Hornby Stationers, Kirkby
             Oswald. Duties included stock control and reordering,
             taking telephone orders and helping with dispatches.

INTERESTS

Acting as Treasurer for the Teens and Twenties Group and helping
to organise their fund-raising events in aid of local charities.

REASONS FOR APPLYING FOR THIS POST

I enjoyed my vacational work at Hornby's and would now like to
see permanent employment in a similar environment. Hornby's
was supplied by The Paper Mountain and I therefore have some
knowledge of quality standards set by your firm. My experience in
computerised systems includes BookSharp, MegaSheet and Qual 50
and I feel confident I could take on the training necessary to
become proficient in operating WISE programs.

Fig. 22. Karen Dukes' CV.

Karen makes it clear why she wants to join the firm and shows she has a basic knowledge of the type of business Mr Fisher runs. Although she has no experience in WISE programs she has listed those she has already mastered which implies she would not find it difficult to learn another.

Comments on Margaret's CV

Margaret and her husband have a young son. She has purposely not drawn attention to this as she knows from previous experience employers are reluctant to take on mothers with young children. She has chosen to put her personal profile at the focal point emphasising her computer experience, and followed this with her qualifications which show she is motivated to continue her learning. She has also included her date of birth as part of her personal details rather than highlighting it separately.

By slipping her working experience down the page, Margaret manages to reduce the impact of her career break. By stressing she was still actively engaged in work orientated activities during this period, she reduces this impact further. The details of her previous jobs give a good indication of the size of her employers' businesses and the type of responsibilities and skills she needed.

Margaret was pleased to get her CV onto one page, but in doing so she has not been able to bring out her reasons for wanting to work in the wholesale stationery business. She will need to deal with this in her covering letter.

Comments on James' CV

James is not from Northmorland. He came from a large family struggling to make ends meet in an area of high unemployment in the East Midlands. He had little incentive to make anything of himself until he joined the Army.

He met and married his wife while they were both on tour in Germany and she returned to settle in Northmorland after their marriage and the birth of their first child. James decided not to re-enlist at the end of his second term of service and is now set on finding employment as soon as possible in their new home area.

James prefers to concentrate his key skills at the focal point of his CV to emphasise the qualities he can offer. Although his experience and training in the Army have been excellent, he is conscious he has been out of Civvy Street for 15 years and has to some extent lost touch with the commercial world. It is for this reason he has also enrolled to take the RSA course at evening classes.

He has purposely made reference to his wife and family to emphasise his commitment to them and his desire to be employed locally.

CURRICULUM VITAE

Margaret Baker
7 Long Barrow Lane
Kirkby Oswald
Northmorland TU10 9SF
Tel: 01989 93645
Born: 11 February 1958

PERSONAL PROFILE

An enthusiastic, conscientious person, with 8 years experience in computerised bookkeeping, including WISE programs, I am now seeking full-time employment with a local business after taking a career break.

QUALIFICATIONS

1974 O Level: 6 subjects including English and Maths
1997 Year 3 of Accounting Technicians Course
(Years 1 & 2 passed)

PREVIOUS EXPERIENCE

1993-2000 Family commitments. Also provided stand-in bookkeeping and secretarial services for my husband's business.

1987-93 ASSISTANT ADMINISTRATOR, Croesus Unit Trusts Ltd. Croesus House, Ellenby.
Duties included: assisting with accounting functions relating to 16 Unit Trusts, 12 Offshore Funds and 20 External clients; ensuring deadlines were met for completion of accounts; verifying computer data input by junior staff; calculating and validating reports for external clients; completing Treasury returns and liaising with the Inland Revenue; answering queries from customers.

1983-87 WAGES OFFICE SUPERVISOR, Farm Products (Ellenby) Ltd. Low Flatts Industrial Estate, Ellenby.
Duties included: calculating and distributing weekly wages for 150 operatives using both manual and later computerised systems; assisting Accountant in preparing departmental budgets; supervising 4 wages clerks and liaising with senior management on bonus payment systems.

1979-83 ACCOUNTING CLERK/BOOKKEEPER, Rapide Response Agency, Sydney, Australia.
Short-term contract work with a variety of commercial enterprises including a wholesale book company.

1976-79 CLERK/TYPIST for a firm of local solicitors.

INTERESTS

Treasurer for the Church Appeal Committee set up in 1996.
Co-ordinator for the Kirkby Oswald Annual Town Festival since 1995.

Fig. 23. Margaret Baker's CV.

JAMES WINSTON FREEMAN

17 Carmelite Close
Kirkby Oswald
Northmorland TU10 2PG
Tel: (01989) 93350

KEY SKILLS

Able to adjust to new and challenging situations quickly.
Capable of using a range of computerised record systems.
Good communication skills at all levels.
Able to work under pressure and meet deadlines.
Capable of achieving consistently high levels of accuracy.
Able to accept responsibility and to work without supervision.

EXPERIENCE

For the past fifteen years I have been a serving soldier with the
2nd Battalion the Westfordshire Regiment, rising through the ranks to
become Company Quartermaster Sergeant in 1993 responsible for the
distribution and control of stores amounting to £2.5m using
computerised record systems.

During this time I was responsible for the administration of a
company of 100 men and worked directly to the Company Sergeant
Major.

Prior to joining the Army in 1985, I worked on building sites and
was a warehouseman with a paper factory for two years.

QUALIFICATIONS AND TRAINING

1980 CSE – 4 Subjects (Grade 1)
1987 Army Education Promotion Certificate
1992 Army Advanced Education Promotion Certificate
1993 Army Bookkeeping and Stock Accounts Course

PERSONAL DETAILS

Date of birth: 29 July 1964   Health: Excellent
Married   Children: 3

INTERESTS

At the moment I am concentrating on the family, having served
with the Battalion in several tours abroad. I am also studying RSA
Accounting at Evening Classes at Ellendale College.

REASONS FOR APPLYING

I understand from articles in the business pages of the local press
that The Paper Mountain is a go-ahead firm, and I feel the skills I have
acquired during my Army service could be put to good use.

Fig. 24. James Freeman's CV.

He has also shown he has taken the trouble to keep abreast of local business news in the press, and has seen the potential in the job offered by The Paper Mountain.

ACTION CHECKLIST

● Understand the difference between information you use on an application form and what you select for a CV.

● Identify which format suits your personal circumstances best.

● Aim to keep your CV to a single page or two at the most.

● Identify your main strength for the focal point of the first page.

● Aim for a positive and interesting writing style.

● Include only facets of your life relevant to the job.

● Aim for the 'looks good' factor with a typed or printed final version.

7

Using the Phone

WHY YOU MIGHT HAVE TO USE THE PHONE

Some people have great trouble putting themselves across over the phone. They can chat away for hours with their friends, but as soon as they have to make a formal call they go to pieces.

Often the sheer effort involved in getting in touch with the right person can be unsettling: telephonists who gabble or answer like robots; off-putting musical interludes while you wait to be connected; having to be re-directed to someone who knows nothing about why you are calling – these all contrive to prevent you giving a good account of yourself.

However much you might want to avoid using the phone, there are occasions when you must, such as when an advertisement asks you to contact someone to discuss the job, or where you are asked to request further details.

There are both advantages and disadvantages to telephone conversations.

Advantages

- You can gain access to information quicker than by writing.
- You can raise any queries straightaway.
- You may be better at putting yourself across orally than face-to-face or on paper.

Disadvantages

- The initial contact might be the only chance you get to 'sell' yourself to your prospective employer.
- If you 'fluff' your lines at the beginning, you may not be able to rectify the situation before the end.
- You might have an incomprehensible accent or speech impediment which the telephone tends to emphasise.

PREPARING YOURSELF

If you are unhappy about using the phone on formal occasions, good preparation is the answer. It will not take away all the stress, but it helps keep it under control.

Materials and equipment
Buy a small lined notebook, preferably spiral bound so it lies flat and doesn't close while you are trying to write one-handed. Use alternate lines and black ink to make your writing stand out clearly. Write in capitals if it helps.

Preparing what to say
Write the telephone number of the firm at the top of the page together with the name of the person you want to speak to and their title, if you know it.

If you are answering an advert, list the job title and any reference you might have been asked to quote.

On a fresh page make a list of what you want to say under bold, clear headings which are easy to read while you are making the call. Keep headings simple. Leave spaces between them so you can write in the answers as you go along, or start a new page for each if you think you might be given a detailed reply.

If you are answering an advert, phone when you are asked to. If there is no time specified, or you are cold-calling, avoid Monday mornings or Friday afternoons: no one will be in the right frame of mind to deal with you. The best times are between 10.00 am and noon, and 2.00 pm and 3.00 pm.

Always be mentally prepared to leave a message if the person you want to speak to is unavailable. If necessary write down what you want to say beforehand so you don't find yourself lost for words if the situation arises.

And finally, make sure your pen works and you have sufficient change or an adequate supply of phone cards if you have to use a public call box.

MAKING THE CALL

Before you begin
If you are nervous about phone calls, try the following method to help you through.

● If you are at home, sit down and make yourself comfortable.

● If you are in a call box, choose one which is not the centre of frenzied activity.

- Clear a space in front of you for your note pad so it does not fall on the floor as you write.

- Have your pen to hand.

- Read through your notes to have the 'feel' of them before you start the conversation.

- Take several deep breaths to clear your head before you start.

The call itself

As soon as you make the connection be mentally prepared for someone to answer at any time.

- Listen to what is said – check if you did not hear anything clearly.

- If you get through to a switchboard, ask for the person you want to speak to. Be prepared to be referred to someone else.

- Listen carefully to the information you are given about what is happening if you are being redirected.

- Once you are through announce who you are and why you are calling.

- Answer any questions about your enquiry in a friendly manner. Sound interested and interesting, and *smile* while you speak. This gives a pleasing effect over the phone.

- Speak slightly slower than usual.

- Try not to waffle – keep to the point.

- Make notes of anything important at the time so you do not forget precise details by the end of the call.

- If you are uncertain about any information you are given, explain your uncertainty and ask for the details to be repeated.

- Finish off by thanking the person for taking the time and trouble to talk to you.

Afterwards

If you intend to make a series of calls, don't be tempted to run through them all one after the other. After each call, read through the notes you made and add any other details you remember. This way you won't find yourself in a hopeless muddle at the end.

Afterwards, transfer the notes into your Job Record File together with the advertisement, if there is one, and write up your Progress Sheet.

COLD-CALLING OVER THE PHONE

To do this you must be confident that:

● you can handle a telephone conversation well

● you can hold an informed conversation about the products or services of the firm you have targeted

● you have some idea about the type of job you are looking for and the likelihood that this exists within the organisation

● you have a comprehensive list of your skills and experience at your fingertips.

Remember the earlier advice about the best times to call and have any relevant personal details to hand.

The purpose of your call

The aim is not to be offered a job on the spot – which won't happen anyway: it is to whet a prospective employer's appetite to know more about you. This means you might be asked to send in a CV, or to make an appointment to meet face-to-face to take the discussion a few steps further.

If you get either of these opportunities, accept them unhesitatingly. Don't try to negotiate an alternative or you may find the offer is withdrawn altogether.

Meeting resistance

If you find your approach is producing a negative response take the initiative: offer to send in your CV or ask to make an appointment to discuss the possibility of any openings being available in the future. If you still come up against a brick wall, withdraw gracefully. There is no point in persisting once you sense hostility: to carry on will simply increase the level of antagonism and you are unlikely to achieve anything by doing this.

AN EXAMPLE TO STUDY V

This example uses the advertisement for a part-time telemarketing executive – Figure 11 (6) on page 63.

Michael Evans (54)

Michael is married with a successful career in sales both on the road and over the phone. His last full-time job was in telemarketing, cold-calling on businesses to persuade them to take out advertising space in a regional newspaper, a job which came easily to him.

A year ago his wife's health failed and her condition quickly deteriorated. It became increasingly difficult for Michael to work full-time and fulfil his caring role as well, so he took the conscious decision to resign.

He is now employed on a casual basis with a market research unit carrying out telephone surveys. However, he would prefer to have more regular employment and the opportunity to become a part-time telemarketing executive interests him, particularly the negotiable working hours and the chance to make the role permanent.

There are two areas he is unsure about:

1.   He has no direct experience of selling training, although he has been on several training courses himself.

2.   He meets all the criteria, but he is wary of the first requirement (money motivated). This seems to be aimed at finding someone who puts money before everything else – and this leaves a question mark about the ethics of the company and its marketing strategy.

Keeping these two points in mind, Michael sets about his preparation before phoning Nigel Temple.

Proving the criteria asked for

Michael will not convince a prospective employer he is capable of doing the job just by saying he meets all the criteria in the advertisement. He will have to give examples to prove his case. To do this, he writes down the five criteria as headings, leaving the troublesome first one until last.

Proven success and experience in telemarketing

The relevant word here is 'telemarketing'. It would be a mistake for Michael to concentrate either on the casual work he is doing at the moment or his selling career prior to his last full-time job. These should only be used in a supportive role.

To demonstrate his success, Michael records his target figures over the period he was in telemarketing, along with bonus payments and commission details. Separately, he also writes down a brief description of his present market survey work and how he organises his workload.

A good administrator
This is where Michael can use his previous experience. His Personal Data File provides him with the best examples from his career history to prove his efficiency in keeping records and paperwork. It also gives him the opportunity to mention his role in setting up a local carers support group, although he does not intend to do this until he is satisfied this might be of interest to Nigel and his company.

Mature and able to work with little supervision
Michael's age is an advantage here, and he has plenty of examples from his career history to demonstrate his self-motivation and success rates.

GCSE (Grades A–C) in English Language
Michael has an equivalent O-Level in English and can lift this data straight from his Personal Data File.

Money-motivated and determined to succeed
Michael gives a lot of thought to this heading. Determination to succeed can be demonstrated by his previous performance levels, commission and bonus payments.

Money motivation is a different matter. Most people need money to survive. Now that Michael's earnings have dropped dramatically, he is much more aware of financial pressures than he used to be. To that extent therefore, and the fact he is looking for regular employment, he is money-motivated, but it is not the prime moving force in seeking this job: it's the flexibility which attracts him.

Under these circumstances, Michael decides to concentrate on his desire to succeed and bring in his need for more financial security as a back-up rather than vice-versa.

Reasons for applying for this post
Even though this is not a heading in the advertisement, Michael decides to make space for it in his notes as a useful addition to bring in if necessary.

His personal reasons for wanting the job are not relevant as far as his prospective employer is concerned, so Michael has to identify others which fit the bill.

Because the advert does not give the name of the company, he cannot do any background research on the services they offer. The style of advertisement seems to indicate they are primarily interested in attracting someone who is capable of marketing anything. Training only gets the briefest of mentions but this might be an oversight on the part of the recruiter. Under these circumstances, Michael decides on the following reasons:

- he believes if the product is right, his previous experience will enable him to sell it

- he has always recognised the importance of good quality training in his own career.

Questions he will want to ask

Michael wants to get Nigel talking straightaway about the company, its products and its philosophy so he can adjust his approach accordingly. Mentally he is prepared to go all out for the job or to back off, depending on the sort of answers he gets. To achieve his goal, he sets out the following strategy.

Michael prepares to shape the conversation to meet his own requirements. He begins by giving himself a framework to work in.

Introduction
Introduce myself.
Mention where I saw the advertisement – then straight into –

Directional thrust
Express interest and immediately ask for more details specifically on

- the name of the company
- the size of its operations
- how long the company has been in existence
- the type of training offered.

Note down any queries and raise these immediately.

Impression of company
What impression am I getting?

Decision (1)
Do I want to pursue this application? Yes/No.

If yes
Open general discussion on experience and skills.

Relate these to the job.
Take up conditions of service

- salary and bonuses
- negotiable hours
- what is involved in making the role permanent?

Decision (2)
Do I still want to pursue this application? Yes/No.

If yes
Wrap up any final queries.
Formalise what happens next.

Conclusion
Note down anything relevant about the conversation for future reference.
Put notes and advert into Job Record File.
Bring Progress Sheet up to date.

Michael is now mentally prepared to begin his conversation with Nigel.

AVOIDING LOST OPPORTUNITIES

Cold calling is an art, but using the telephone effectively as a communication medium is a skill – and an increasingly essential skill.

If you are put off applying for jobs because the initial contact has to be made by phone, you could be losing out on applying for a job which is right for you. You may overcome your reluctance by using the thorough preparation technique suggested earlier in the chapter – and lots of practice. But if your nervousness is not so easily overcome, then it may be worthwhile considering taking a telephone skills course. Your local Jobcentre may be able to help you find a suitable course in your area.

ACTION CHECKLIST

● Research the background of the company or organisation you intend to contact.

● Know who you want to speak to, or an alternative if this person is not available.

● Have the job title and any reference quoted on hand.

- Have pen and paper ready to jot down information.

- Choose the right time to make the call.

- Have a prepared list of questions written down with space set aside for the answers.

- Devise a structured series of optional questions to move the conversation forward.

- Know when and how to close the call.

8

Making 'On Spec' Visits

WHEN THESE CAN BE USEFUL

'Dropping in' on employers is a chancy business. Some companies may not let you past the gate unless you have already been cleared as a visitor, or have a pass. But there are occasions when the 'on spec' approach pays dividends.

If you live close to a small industrial estate or business park, and you are looking for a job which could be offered by several employers – general office work for instance – you can set off armed with your CV and a smile and aim to cover all the businesses in one day.

'On spec' visits are also useful in rural areas where you are aiming for a local employer. The chances are you are already known by sight, or on a casual basis. Introducing yourself as a job-hunter may give you the advantage over someone who does not make personal contact.

Advantages of 'on spec' visits

From your point of view there are several advantages.

1. *You can see the working environment first*
    When you send off a letter, CV or an application form, you often have no idea of the working environment you are letting yourself in for. It can sometimes come as something of a shock when you attend the interview. Having a good look at the place can help you decide *before* you apply whether you want to take your application further or not.

2. *You can evaluate the way the organisation is run*
    A reception or waiting area can tell you a lot about how the company wants to be seen by outsiders. It does not have to be potted palms and plush carpets, or receptionists looking like models off the front covers of women's fashion magazines, for you to recognise a firm with high standards. One the other hand, grubby glass, corridors filled with furniture or equipment, harassed-looking staff, phones ringing and not being answered, leave a very different impression.

3. *The visit can turn into an interview*
It is possible you could be seen as a potential employee. A job opening may have just occurred, or is expected to occur shortly. With
recruitment such an expensive business, employers are keen to find
ways of reducing costs. Your enterprise could well be rewarded.

4. *Some employers find it harder to turn away prospective job-hunters
from the premises*
Even if there is no likelihood of a job becoming immediately available,
you may be given the opportunity to speak to someone who is prepared
to keep you in mind in future.

Disadvantages of 'on spec' visits
You have to be prepared for the down side of cold-calling.

1. *You only have one shot at it*
Like a phone call, if you fluff it, there is no way you are going to be
able to call again and redeem yourself.

2. *You may not find anyone available to see you*
This is the most likely outcome. If no one is expecting you, there is a
good chance the relevant person is away, in a meeting, or just about to
catch a train.

3. *You may antagonise people by dropping in without an appointment*
Don't underestimate the irritation level this can cause. Apologise at
reception straightaway and ask if anyone would be able to see you
despite your lack of a prior appointment. You may not succeed, but you
could be given the opportunity of being invited back another time.

4. *You may not have the confidence to cold-call effectively*
If you do not think this approach will work for you, then *don't* use it.

PREPARING TO MAKE A COLD-CALL

You must treat an 'on spec' visit as you would any full-blown interview: it
has the potential to become one and you can't afford to be caught out. This
means thorough preparation is essential.

Personal preparation
Brush up on your interview technique
This is an absolute must. There are plenty of books offering good advice on

this subject (see the author's *Passing that Interview*) if you feel you are a bit rusty. If not, remind yourself of your behavioural habits and the four areas most likely to let you down. These are:

1. **Nervous mannerisms:** shuffling in your seat; twining your fingers round each other or your legs round the chair; biting your lip; foot 'bouncing' after crossing your legs; scratching your ears, nose, chin or neck, or repeatedly tossing your head.

2. **Irritating habits:** sniffing repeatedly, picking your nails; fiddling with a pen or jewellery, or jangling coins in your pocket.

3. **Negative body language and bad posture:** walking with your head down; bursting into a room grinning inanely; ignoring a proffered hand; giving a pump-handle or wet fish handshake; sitting like a sack of potatoes; leaning back nonchalantly as though you owned the place; sitting on the edge of your seat; gripping the arms of the chair; crossing your arms defensively in front of you; or fixing your eyes anywhere but on the speaker.

4. **Poor speech (quality or content):** mumbling; swearing; talking too fast; using trendy phrases; pomposity; putting your hand in front of your mouth while you're talking; using meaningless phrases such as 'you know', or 'like I said'.

Dress for the occasion
You should look good from top to toe. This means:

- clean, well-groomed hair kept well out of your eyes
- properly adjusted spectacles, not broken or amateurishly mended – and never sunglasses
- clean teeth and fresh breath
- hands should be clean and fingernails should not be ragged or dirty
- clothes should be neat, tidy, clean and well-fitting
- shoes should be clean and well-maintained
- the back view should look as good as the front
- for he-man types, well-trimmed beards and moustaches, otherwise regardless of fashion, be clean-shaven.

You should also avoid:

- if you are female, carrying an outsized handbag which makes you look like a plumber's mate

- wearing too much jewellery, or any badge which might have a religious, political or other contentious meaning

- wearing a watch which 'bleeps' on the hour which can be very distracting

- using paper tissues as handkerchiefs – they often become messy shreds in pockets

- wearing too much perfume or after-shave which can be over-powering

- using highly scented hairspray for the same reason

- having body odour – there's no excuse for it.

Taking what you need

This is where an all-purpose CV can come in useful. Take sufficient copies so you can leave one behind for reference purposes at each venue if necessary, and a writing pad so that you can complete a brief covering letter to express your interest in joining the company – and why.

Your Personal Data File might also come in handy, especially if you are asked to complete an application form on the spot. This saves you having to take the form away, thereby losing the impact of your visit. Take a small pad with you for rough work and a pen with black ink.

Research on the company

This is vital. Most employers want to feel prospective employees are interested in the organisation prepared to pay them. Even small businesses set high standards in quality products and customer care and go to some lengths to project the right image. They naturally like to feel they are getting their message across. Being able to comment on some positive aspect of a company's activities produces a 'feel good' factor which should always work to your advantage.

Sources of information
For larger companies, *The Kompass Register, Who Owns Whom* and *Kelly's Business Directory* are all excellent sources of information available at most libraries. There are also annual reports which can be obtained from the company secretary or customer services departments in advance. Firms are usually only too happy to let you have a copy. Features in the business pages of the national dailies are also useful.

If you are looking at a small-scale local business, you can find out what image they are projecting by keeping an eye open for their adverts on television, in local newspapers, cinemas and local radio. The business section of the local paper can also provide you with interesting snippets of information.

Personal contacts with someone already employed by the organisation should not be ignored either. As mentioned in Chapter 3, such contacts can be extremely useful. They often have advance knowledge of when and where certain jobs are likely to become available. They can also provide additional information about the goods or services offered by a firm and the sort of management style and working conditions which operate.

Make sure you know the size of the organisation, the range of products or services they offer, and where you think your skills and experience could be used by them.

Keeping the information

The best way to keep your research in easily accessible and transportable form is to reduce it to key facts written down as headings on 'flash' cards. Stationers or printers often have a variety of off-cuts available which are ideal for this purpose. The cards should be small enough to fit comfortably into either a pocket or handbag.

Using 'flash' cards is a quick and easy way of refreshing your memory if you intend to go round several companies one after the other.

You will also need a small notebook to jot down names, telephone numbers or any other relevant information you are given when you make your visit. This information should be transferred to your Job Record File when you get home.

ON ARRIVAL

Presuming you have got past the gate if there is one, go straight to reception, explain who you are and why you are there. If you do not know who is the most appropriate person to ask for, let whoever is on reception suggest who this might be.

You must be prepared to sit and wait if there is the remotest chance of speaking to someone who is willing to see you. Use any waiting time to revise the key information you have on the company and to get the feel of the activity – or lack of it – taking place around you.

If the person you need to speak to is not available, ask if there is anyone else who could.

If this attempt fails and you find yourself up against a stone wall, you have three options:

1. Offer to leave your CV.

2. Ask to complete an application form if this is the usual method of recruitment adopted by the company.

3. If you feel there is no point in pursuing the matter, politely take your leave.

GETTING AN INTERVIEW

The first thing you should do, if you are lucky enough to be given an interview, is to thank your interviewer for seeing you without notice. You don't have to grovel, but you must show that you appreciate the fact they have set aside time for you. You can then launch into your sales pitch. Even if you have already been told there are no vacancies at the moment, the fact you have been given an interview means there is some hope for the future: no one would waste time seeing you if there was no hope at all.

Interviews which are not pre-arranged are likely to take the form of a discussion. Because of this it is easy to fall into the trap of treating them rather like cosy chats – which they are not. They are still interviews. If your listener doesn't set any format, then make sure you do, otherwise you could find your time's up and you haven't made all the points you wanted to.

Set your stall out as follows:

●   Introduce yourself and state briefly your wish to be considered as a possible employee.

●   Show what you have been able to discover about the business and why you are interested in it.

●   Bring out your skills and experience and relate these to the business and where you feel they could be used.

Unless you are talking to the owner of the business, or a personnel officer who is in a position to act autonomously, it is unlikely you will get an immediate answer. Do make the point of finding out when you are likely to hear anything so that you can make a note of this on your Progress Sheet later.

Sometimes during the interview it might become clear there is no opening for you after all. Perhaps your experience or skills are not quite right. Accept this decision with good grace and use the experience as a learning process. Maybe this is the time to consider getting those skills or experience, particularly if there is any likelihood of openings in the future. More of this in Chapter 10.

DEPARTING

When you leave, irrespective of whether or not you were able to talk to someone, thank everyone for their time and trouble. Don't forget to SMILE. This is important even if you made very little progress and feel thoroughly frustrated. Life has a habit of turning up coincidences. The chances are you could well meet up with these people again in other circumstances. You do not want to be remembered for anything which might put you in a bad light.

If you didn't make much progress, or you feel hurt or angry:

Don't . . .
- give way to your emotions
- take out your anger on other staff
- ever be rude.

Get out your flash cards, read up the details of the next company on your list, and carry on.

ACTION CHECKLIST

- Research the background of the company or organisation you intend to approach.

- Transfer key facts onto 'flash cards' for easy reference.

- Brush up your interview technique.

- Take with you an all-purpose CV to leave if requested.

- Have your Personal Data File with you in case you need to complete an application form.

- Have a structured approach to the interview already planned in your mind to make the best use of your time.

- Know when and how to close the discussion positively.

9

Reviewing Your Progress

If you are in a jobs market where there are more applicants than vacancies, landing a job can take longer than you expected. You may have several applications on the go at once. If your Progress Sheet is up-to-date you can keep track of them, including making enquiries if you expected to hear from an employer and no one has contacted you.

Your Progress Sheet also provides you with another tool – a means of checking your overall progress in the job-hunt – and perhaps to consider whether there is any need to start revising your approach to the task.

Success at this stage of the job search is measured in terms of getting an interview. If the invitation never arrives, you are nowhere near landing a job.

ANALYSING YOUR SUCCESS RATE

Remember success in this context = interviews. Look through your Progress Sheet at what has happened to your applications so far. Are you consistently obtaining interviews? If the answer to this question is 'Yes' then at least you have the consolation of knowing there is nothing wrong with the way you are tackling your applications. The problem obviously now lies elsewhere. There are three possibilities.

1. The type of experience or skills offered by other candidates was better than yours.

2. There may be some aspect of your interview technique which is letting you down and needs brushing up.

3. You may be applying for the wrong sort of job without knowing it and this is only coming over during the course of the interview.

How to unravel which is responsible for your lack of interview success is not within the scope of this book, but if you want to succeed, you will need to concentrate on these other areas of the job search which now appear to be the stumbling blocks.

On the other hand, if you are not receiving any offers of interviews there is some fundamental problem which has to be tackled. Don't carry on in the same way and think this doesn't matter. It does. Something is wrong with your approach and it needs to be tracked down and put right, otherwise you will never succeed.

If you are managing to get some interviews, but not consistently, then this too needs to be looked into: there may be some way of improving on your success rate.

LACK OF SUCCESS

Patterns of failure

The first thing to look for is whether or not you can see any clear pattern emerging from your Progress Sheet which points to a particular weakness. Are your non-successful applications the result of:

- application letters?
- application forms?
- CVs?
- faxed data?
- e-mail or Internet applications?
- 'on spec' calls over the phone?
- 'on spec' visits?
- some of the above?
- all of the above?

If you can see a clear pattern where one type of application has clearly not been successful, then you can set about thinking of ways of improving your product. For instance, if all your application forms let you down, there is a good chance there is something about the way you are completing these which is not selling your skills in the right way. But the problem may lie outside your control. For instance, is the quality of your faxed letter or CV being spoiled at the receiving end? Are your Internet applications falling foul of poor recruitment practices in the organisations you are applying to?

If you find a mixed bag of success or failure with the same type of application then compare those which were successful with those which weren't. See if you can identify anything about the successful applications which gives them the edge over the non-successful. Have you used a particular descriptive phrase or given a good account of your reasons for applying for the job which sounds more attractive? Is there anything about the layout which is more eye-catching? If you are strictly honest with yourself, you can often put your finger on something which either strikes a good chord, or doesn't.

If you are having no success no matter what type of application you use then you may be facing more fundamental problems which have nothing to do with the way you complete your applications.

No success

This can be crushing. What's worse, panic can set in with all sorts of misdirected activity taking place as a result. This leads to even more failure, and eventually to a sense of hopelessness, loss of self-esteem and a rapidly accelerating downward spiral which prevents you from taking control of your life and getting back on your feet. This has to be avoided at all costs.

There are several possible reasons why you are not succeeding.

1. *You have not grasped the basic essentials of putting across your case successfully*
   Are your layouts immediately attractive and eye-catching? Have you kept your information relevant to the job? Have you put your skills and experience in the right context? Have you given the employer any good reason for wanting to employ you? Have you gone for quantity rather than quality? Remember the 'scattergun' approach to job-hunting rarely works.

2. *You are applying for the wrong type of job*
   Are you over-qualified or under-qualified? Are you outside the stated or expected age-range? Have you too much or too little experience? Have you not got the skills being sought, or not enough of them? You must match some of the requirements being sought, even if these are portable skills.

3. *You appear to be a job-hopper at heart*
   Have you gone into too much detail with part-time, casual or temporary jobs which were 'fill-ins' and not part of your intended career pattern? Are you a job-hopper at heart? If so, why not stick to short-term temporary contract work and make a proper career out it?

4. *You appear to be directionless*
   Have you a career history which appears not to know where it is going? Can you identify any threads running through your jobs which could be used to show a logical progression to your career? If you can't, you need to provide evidence to confirm why you believe the direction you

now want to travel in is the right one for you – and your prospective employer.

5. *You are possibly being subjected to prejudice*
Are you applying for jobs with stereotyped gender bias? Are you over 40? Are you from an ethnic minority? Do you live in an area with a bad reputation? Have you some form of disability? Discrimination does occur, but at the application stage it is difficult to prove unless you are in a position to obtain inside information on the recruitment process.

6. *You are not paying sufficient attention to detail*
Are you making your applications in the manner requested? Are you paying attention to the type of information being requested in the advertisement? Is your presentation up to scratch? Remember, you only have a few seconds to make a good impression on a recruiter.

7. *You are consistently selling yourself short or over-selling yourself*
Are you playing down your achievements? Are you giving the impression of being a shrinking violet? Are you implying the business cannot hope to succeed without you? Are you trying to make more of your achievements than you should? Does your application make you sound dull? Does it make you sound pompous? Try to steer a middle course.

REVISING YOUR TACTICS

If you can identify a problem in the way you are presenting yourself don't let it happen again. Review your previous methods and revise what you have been doing until you are satisfied there is an improvement. Never let yourself be content with second best.

If you are genuinely stumped, don't sit around and hope the problem will go away. It won't. Get in touch with the nearest Jobcentre or careers service provider. They will be able to advise you on what's best to meet your particular problem. Working on a problem is always the best way of overcoming it. On page 148 is a questionnaire for you to complete to start the process.

REVIEWING THE SITUATION

Can you answer 'Yes' to the following statements for every application you made which did not result in an interview?

1. My writing is neat and legible.

2. My written layout (or telephone manner) is good.

3. I have used the correct method of making the application.

4. I have used the best examples of my skills and experience gained in the workplace.

5. I have used the best examples of my skills and experience gained in my pastimes.

6. I have emphasised the positive aspects of my experience.

7. I have included only relevant information.

8. I have used the most appropriate paper for the application letter (or CV).

9. My style of writing has produced an attractive and interesting application.

10. I have answered all the above questions honestly and truthfully.

Fig. 25. Use this questionnaire to review the situation.

ACTION CHECKLIST

- Analyse your success rate at regular intervals.
- Identify any patterns of failure linked to a particular type of application.
- Revise your approach if problems exist in specific areas.
- Compare successful with unsuccessful applications if these are in the same format to identify what might have made the difference.
- Question your approach rigorously if you have had no success in any format.
- Take positive action to rectify any weaknesses you identify.

10

Getting Ahead

In a jobs market full of well-qualified or equally experienced competitors, you have to find a way of giving yourself the edge over the others. This does not mean dashing off and enrolling for additional qualifications. Often, additional qualifications only make you over qualified rather than *better* qualified.

GAINING ADDITIONAL SKILLS

Employers are interested in what you can bring to their business, and qualifications alone are not enough. Many graduates leave college or university expecting the world to fall at their feet, and then become resentful when it doesn't. A degree proves you are a good student but says nothing about how you will fare in the world of work. This situation is not helped by an increasing number of graduates coming onto the jobs market with degrees which employers do not recognise as being relevant to the workplace.

What skills?

Skills do not necessarily tie in with qualifications. There are no degrees in:

- leadership
- self-motivation
- good communication
- team building, or the like.

If you have a general degree not linked to a specific profession, to succeed in the jobs market you may need practical skills as well, such as:

- keyboard ability
- competency in information and communication technology
- fluency in one or more languages in a commercial setting
- first aid

- bookkeeping
- advanced driving, or a Large Goods Vehicle (LGV) or Passenger Carrying Vehicle (PCV) licence.

Anyone up against equally experienced candidates has the same problem trying to lift themselves above the general mass of competition. Knowing what additional skills would be useful – in the engineering industry for instance – depends in part on your inside knowledge of the industry, and partly on intuition – where the industry is likely to go in future. Being able to speak and understand Arabic, for instance, might open a whole new range of opportunities. The same could be said of learning any language of the European Union, and being able to understand and speak it fluently within the context of your own sphere of work.

The massive influx of information and communication technology into almost every part of our everyday lives means that no matter what job you go for you will need to be computer literate.

Computer literacy does not mean being able to play the latest computer game up to Level 85 – or at the other end of the spectrum being able to program in the latest computer language: it means being able to understand the uses of a computerised information system within an industrial or commercial context.

There are now very few jobs which rely solely on the pen and paper approach. Even quite small businesses have computerised cash tills and stocktaking; garages and specialist spare parts stockists operate on the same basis; banks and building societies have very sophisticated information systems; so do many offices where not just the payroll is on computer but personnel files as well; and most industries have been running on computer technology for years. There has been an explosion in the use of the Internet over the last five years and many organisations have their own Intranet systems as well.

If you believe your main problem is too many candidates with broadly similar qualifications or skills as your own, think how you could give yourself the advantage over them, and what skills you would need to develop.

Acquiring additional skills
Once you have identified the relevant skills you are looking for, you can take practical steps towards getting them.

Some skills, such as language and basic office skills, are available in the form of courses at local colleges. To see what is on offer, ask for their latest prospectus.

Information and communication technology skills are now almost universally required or accepted as the norm. With most school children now computer literate, if you are a mature applicant who missed out on the technological revolution you cannot afford to ignore this trend. There is a whole range of courses to meet different needs. Contact your local colleges or WEA, or sample what's on offer from training providers specialising in the latest technology. Shop around and find out more.

First aid courses are organised by the Red Cross or St John Ambulance and these organisations are listed in *The Phone Book*.

More specialised business skills may be available from local training providers. These are listed under 'Training Services' in The *Yellow Pages*. However, it is not always clear from individual entries what sort of training is on offer. Up until April 2001, you can contact your nearest Training and Enterprise Council (TEC) or Local Enteprise Company (LEC) in Scotland for help. After April 2001 the training functions of TECs are being transferred to 47 local Learning and Skills Councils (LSCs) in England organised to reflect travel-to-work and travel-to-learn areas. The Scottish LECs are not being affected by this change, although they may be in the future. The enterprise side of the TECs has already been hived off and is now known as the Small Business Service. This is now operated by the existing Business Link structure with effect from April 2000.

Many language skills providers and correspondence colleges advertise their courses in the national press. If you want a comprehensive list of accredited correspondence colleges contact:

Open and Distance Learning Quality Council
16 Park Crescent,
London W1H 4AH

If you are unsure who to contact, get in touch with your local Jobcentre first. You can then discuss your training needs and let them direct you to the most appropriate provider.

BROADENING YOUR HORIZONS

Travelling abroad

This is a popular choice for young people: glamorous sounding places, a good social life, mixing with people your own age. Travelling in this way, however, is not going to add anything to your range of work-skills. Having a good time does not qualify you to become good at a job.

If you are going to gain tangible results from travelling abroad, you have to do more than just travel – you have to travel with a definite purpose, and it has to be the sort of travelling you would not associate with taking a holiday.

Taking a year out

There are an increasing number of school-leavers who take a year away from academic studies before beginning their college or university courses. Many higher education institutions find that students who do this have distinct advantages over those who start their courses straight from school. Year-out students on the whole are:

● clearer about the type of course they want to take and why they want to take it

● maturer in their approach to their studies

● usually better motivated and more capable of organising their time effectively; and consequently

● usually do better academically.

The definitive book on this subject must be *A Year Between* by the Central Bureau for Educational Visits and Exchanges. It is available in main libraries and should be obligatory reading for anyone contemplating taking a year out. There is no aspect it does not cover. Look, too, at Nick Vandome's excellent *Spending a Year Abroad* in the How To series.

Employers' reactions to the year out are generally favourable, provided this is taken *before* going on to higher education, and is aimed at developing skills and experience. They are less enthusiastic about students who take a year out *after* completing their studies unless the placement was relevant and followed on naturally from their course. If it does not fit into this category, the assumption is you just want to have a good time instead of getting down to the business of finding a job.

Community work or helping a charity

There are plenty of opportunities for anyone of any age, or any background, to brush up or acquire new skills by offering to help community projects or local charities.

If you have been out of the job market for some time, perhaps because you have been bringing up a family, looking after an elderly relative, or because you have lost your job, you may lack confidence. Perhaps all you feel you have to offer is your time. Don't use this as an excuse for not making the effort. Time is often what is most needed.

Meeting other people or helping those in less fortunate circumstances can often put your own life into a better perspective. Involvement often brings with it an increased sense of self-worth as confidence returns. Once your confidence is in place, other abilities can emerge: an improvement in communication skills; the ability to work as one of a team; leadership skills; and a willingness to take on more demanding tasks, such as large-scale fund-raising, organising outings or taking on a treasurership or secretarial role. These are all useful portable skills.

Even if you are already in employment and seeking new work, having these extra activities not only gives a prospective employer a fuller picture of the sort of person you are, but also demonstrates you have a broader range of skills than those you have simply acquired in the workplace.

Temporary or part-time employment

This is a useful way of getting work experience if you have not been employed, or have had a career break for any reason.

Temporary posts are usually easier to find because most people are looking for more permanent employment, even on a part-time basis. But pick your casual employment with care so that it provides a genuine learning process to help you in future. This way, you will be able to explain your choice rationally when applying for full-time posts. For instance, being a deck-chair attendant can be relevant if you want to gain experience in meeting people and handling money, whereas being a street cleaner would not.

Part-time work is ideal for feeling your way back into the world of work. You also have the benefit of learning how the technological revolution has changed almost every working environment. Again, pick your part-time job carefully so that it can lead on naturally to a full-time post with similar skills.

Shadowing

This is the adult version of a work experience placement. It is unpaid, and you simply 'shadow' someone during the course of their work and see what is involved.

Shadowing allows you to appreciate the complexities of a job and gives you the opportunity of discussing various aspects of it with the person doing it. This can be an excellent learning process.

Shadowing is particularly useful if you are thinking about trying something different, or changing your career direction. You may be able to organise a placement through a local branch of a professional or trade association; or through personal connections; or by asking the personnel section of an organisation if it would be possible. There's nothing lost by asking.

Finding jobs linked to hobbies

If you are looking for a change of direction, using your hobbies as a lever into a new job market is another possibility.

You already know from your Personal Data File what skills you have acquired from your hobbies. These might be very different from those you acquired at work. Are your hobbies' skills portable skills? What sort of jobs might be open to you with these skills? What other jobs would be open to you if you built on these skills further? If you don't know the answers to these questions, contact your local Jobcentre, careers service provider, TEC or after April 2001, your local LSC, and discuss these ideas with them. Some skills are in short supply and those you have from your hobbies might be among them.

THE CHANGING JOBS MARKET

Undoubtedly, the last few years have seen tremendous changes in the jobs market: the easing of trade barriers; the opening up of Eastern Europe; and the effects of more rapid communication systems and modern technology on almost every aspect of our lives.

Both the public and private sectors are having to change their management structures. Those who do not, go under.

Job content is changing too. In the past many jobs were too narrow in their approach. Businesses can no longer afford to have employees with limited abilities and reluctance to take on other tasks – they must be 'multi-skilled'. And it isn't only a broader base of skills which is being looked for – it is a broader set of attitudes as well. Employees have to be prepared to be flexible in their jobs, to take more responsibility for what they do, and be prepared to take on new challenges.

It bears repeating – we all have more skills than we give ourselves credit for. Now is the time to discover them.

ACTION CHECKLIST

- Identify skills you need to improve your employability.

- Research skills providers to meet your identified needs.

- Take action to acquire the necessary skills.

- Identify ways to broaden your life experiences to enhance your job opportunities.

- Keep abreast of changes in the jobs market and what these mean in terms of job opportunities for you.

- Adapt your job search to meet changes.

- Keep all your options open.

Glossary

Apex Trust: a registered charity offering employment advice to ex-offenders.

body language: the conscious or unconscious signals given to others by using certain gestures, facial expressions and body movements.

Business Link: a Department of Trade and Industry initiative for enterprise advice services operating through local delivery companies.

career history: the record of your working life comprising job titles, key tasks and responsibilities, names and addresses of employers and dates when employed.

Chartered Institute of Personnel and Development (CIPD): the professional body for personnel and training officers in the UK and the Republic of Ireland.

curriculum vitae (CV): a resumé of personal details, interests and previous employment often requested *in lieu* of an application form.

early retirement (see also redundancy): the bringing forward of a retirement date or age to reduce staff numbers in an organisation.

e-mail: the sending of information to individuals or organisations with e-mail addresses using world wide computer links sharing a common computer language.

halo effect: the enhancement of your chances of success brought about by a single aspect of your appearance or presentation meeting with approval.

hidden agenda: the true reason behind a course of action which is known only to a limited number of people.

Internet: the world wide computer network which allows users to communicate directly with one another through **e-mail** and provides access to information available on **Web sites**.

Intranet: an organisation's internal Web network used for information, processing and management purposes secure from public external access.

key tasks: the main duties involved in carrying out a job.

Learning and Skills Councils (LSCs): 47 locally based organisations set up by the Department for Education and Employment to co-ordinate post-16 learning and workforce development after April 2001.

Local Enterprise Companies (LECs): government funded agencies run by local industrialists and other employers responsible for coordinating training and enteprise projects in Scotland.

National Association for the Care and Resettlement of Offenders (NACRO): a national registered charity assisting with the rehabilitation of offenders into the community.

on-target earnings (OTE): the salary on offer if the sales targets are met.

portable skills: special talents or abilities which you can adapt or reshape to use in different ways in different environments.

private sector: that part of the country's economy which is owned and operated by private individuals and firms.

public sector: that part of the economy which includes government financed industry and the social services, including the health service, government departments and local government.

recruitment agencies: privately run businesses operating to provide staff for clients.

redundancy: the loss of a job when this is no longer required by the employing company or organisation.

skills: practical abilities or cleverness needed to carry out a job competently and effectively.

Small Business Service: agencies of the Department of Trade and Industry with local links designed to provide a one-stop shop for the delivery of business support services.

Training and Enterprise Council (TEC): government funded agencies run by local industrialists and other employers responsible for coordinating government training projects in England until March 2001.

transferable skills: see **portable skills**.

vetting procedures: the checking of police and other agency records to gauge the suitability of someone applying for a job.

Web site: a store of information on the **Internet** accessed through the computer network by keying in a unique address dedicated to that site.

work experience: the time you spend in a working environment acquiring skills and knowledge of working practices.

Further Information

USEFUL ADDRESSES

Apex Trust, St Alphage House, Wingate Annexe, 2 Fore Street, London EC2Y 5DA. Tel: (020) 7638 5931; Fax: (020) 7638 5977; e-mail: apexho@globalnet.co.uk

Commission for Racial Equality, Elliot House, 10–12 Allington Street, London SW1E 5EH. Tel: (020) 7828 7022; e-mail: info@cre.gov.uk; Website: www.cre.gov.uk

Disability Rights Commission, 7th Floor, 222 Grays Inn Road, London WC1X 8HL. Tel: (020) 7211 3000; Fax (020) 7211 4141; ; Minicom; (020) 7211 4037; e-mail: enquiry@drc-gb.org; Website: www.drc-gb.org

Employment Agency Standards Office, Department of Trade and Industry, 1 Victoria Street, London SW1H 0ET. Tel: (0645) 555 105 (local rates apply); Fax: (020) 7215 2636; e-mail: mailbox.ir2@irdv.dti.gov.uk; Website: www.dti.gov.uk/er

Equal Opportunities Commission, Overseas House, Quay Street, Manchester M3 3HN. Tel: (0161) 833 9244; e-mail: info@eoc.org.uk; Website: www.eoc.org.uk

National Association for the Care and Resettlement of Offenders (NACRO), 169 Clapham Road, London SW9 0PU. Tel: (020) 7582 6500; Fax: (020) 7735 4666

National Institute of Adult Continuing Education (NIACE), 21 De Montfort Street, Leicester LE1 7GE. Tel: (0116) 255 1451; e-mail: niace@niace.org.uk; Website: www.niace.org.uk

National Open College Network, NOCN Office, University of Derby, Kedleston Road, Derby, DE22 1GB. Tel: (01332) 622712; Fax: (01332) 622734; e-mail: nocn@derby.ac.uk; Website for details of all local branches: www.nocn.ac.uk

Open and Distance Learning Quality Council, 16 Park Crescent, London W1H 4AH. Tel: (020) 7612 7090; Fax: (020) 7612 7092; e-mail: oalqc@dial.pipex.com; Website:http://www.odlqc.org.uk/odlqc.

Workers Educational Association, Temple House, 17 Victoria Park Square, London E2 9PB. Tel: (020) 8983 1515; Fax: (020) 8983 4840; e-mail: info@wea.org.uk; Website: www.wea.org.uk

FURTHER READING

Back to Work, Gemma O'Connor (Optima).
Best Companies for Women, Scarlett McGwire (Pandora).
CVs and Written Applications, Judy Skeats (Ward Lock).
Electronic Job Search Revolution, Joyce Kennedy and Thomas Morrow (Wiley).
Electronic Resume Revolution, Joyce Kennedy and Thomas Morrow (Wiley).
Enhancing Your Employability, Roderic Ashley (How To Books, 1998)
Getting a Better Job, John Courtis (CIPD).
Getting a Job Abroad, Roger Jones (How To Books, 5th edition, 1999).
Getting a Job in America, Roger Jones (How To Books, 5th edition 1998).
Getting a Job in Australia, Nick Vandome (How To Books, 3rd edition 1997).
Getting a Job in Europe, Mark Hempshell (How To Books, 4th edition 1999).
Getting That Job, Joan Fletcher (How To Books, 4th edition 1997).
Getting the Right Job, Judy Skeats (Ward Lock).
How to Get That Job After 45, Julie Bayley (Kogan Page).
How to Write a Winning CV, Alan Jones (Hutchinson).
How You Can Get That Job!, Rebecca Corfield (Kogan Page).
Making a Comeback, Margaret Korving (Hutchinson).
The Perfect CV, Tom Jackson (Piatkus).
Passing That Interview, Judith Johnstone (How To Books, 5th edition 1999).
Planning a New Career, Judith Johnstone (How To Books, 3rd edition 1999).
Preparing Your Own CV, Rebecca Corfield (Kogan Page).
Returning to Work, Alex Reed (Kogan Page).
Spending a Year Abroad, Nick Vandome (How To Books, 4th edition 1999).
Taking a Year Off, Val Butcher and Chris Swanson (Trotman).
Taking Control of Your Own Career, Barbara Buffton (How To Books, 1999)
Telephone Skills, Patrick Forsyth (CIPD).
The Ultimate CV for Managers and Professionals, Rachel Bishop-Firth (How To Books 2000).
Using the Internet. Graham Jones (How To Books 4th edition, 2000).
Writing a CV That Works, Paul McGee (How To Books, 2nd edition 1997).
A Year Between, (Central Bureau for Educational Visits and Exchanges).
Your First Job, Anne Page (Kogan Page).

Index